TEACHER PROFESSIONALISM DURING THE PANDEMIC

This insightful book uniquely charts the events, experiences and challenges faced by teachers during and beyond the COVID-19 pandemic including periods of national lockdowns and school closures.

Research-based and evidence informed, this key title explores the multiple media outputs created by teachers in a variety of different socio-economic contexts. The authors reflect on their stories through a series of themed analyses, as well as describing and discussing key issues related to the enactment of teacher professionalism in challenging times.

With fascinating vignettes and interview extracts that reinforce the idea that teachers can manage rather than survive, this book unveils a strong sense of moral purpose, professional identity, commitment, care and resilience. It will be of interest to teachers, head teachers and teacher educators internationally.

Christopher Day is Professor of Education in the School of Education, University of Nottingham, UK, and Professor of Educational Leadership and Management in the University of Sydney, Australia. He is a Founder of the International Study Association on Teachers and Teaching (ISATT), leader of the International School Principalship Project (ISSPP), and his latest books are *School-University Partnerships in Action: The Promise of Change* (2021) and *Teachers' Worlds' and Work: Understanding Complexity, Building Quality* (2017).

Helen Victoria Smith is Assistant Professor in the School of Education, University of Nottingham, UK, where she is course leader and English lead for the Primary PGCE.

Ruth Graham is an Assistant Professor at The University of Nottingham, UK. She joined the research project in 2021, following her own experience as a teacher and subject lead within a primary school during the pandemic.

Despoina Athanasiadou is a PhD candidate in the School of Education, University of Nottingham, UK. She is a part-time tutor for the Educational Leadership and Management MA programme.

'This is a book packed full of irresistibly powerful stories from teachers as they faced the consequences of the pandemic. We hear of doubts, fears and exhaustion but ultimately this is a book that emphasises hope and the power of teacher collegiality. A great reminder of all that our profession stands for.'

Dame Alison Peacock, Chief Executive Chartered College of Teaching, UK

'This insightful, scholarly book deserves full attention from anyone who cares deeply about improving the work and lives of teachers and enabling them to remain enthusiastic, dedicated and passionate about the difference that they strive to make in their daily classrooms. Using real stories from real teachers in real schools, the authors remind us how physically, intellectually and emotionally challenging the teaching profession is and how deeply and profoundly the unprecedented pandemic has tested the strengths of teachers' professionalism and capacity to serve. However, and perhaps most importantly, these stories also give us hope and promise because, in many ways, they reinforce an old truth about teachers and teaching: although schools alone cannot address the structural disruptions caused by the pandemic, in such testing times, they represent an oasis of hope where many knowledgeable, committed and caring teachers have learned to give their best to inspire the learning and achievement of young minds. As such, this book represents a new landmark in the continuous building of knowledge space on *why* and *how* teachers matter.'

Qing Gu, Director, UCL Centre for Educational Leadership, UCL Institute of Education, UK

'This book is impressive and timely. It makes a compelling case of how teachers responded to one of the most difficult challenges of their lives. Based on rich longitudinal empirical evidence, *Teacher Professionalism During the Pandemic: Resilience, Courage and Care* shows the complexity and multi-dimensionality of teaching and the significance of relationships in teachers' work and wellbeing. It presents inspiring stories of courage, commitment and hope that clearly demonstrate who teachers are, what they do and why. This is a valuable contribution to the field and a must-read book for all those who are interested in better understanding teachers' work and lives.'

Maria Assunção Flores, Editor, European Journal of Teacher Education, University of Minho, Portugal

'Mostly, it seems, when addressing the effects of COVID-19 on education only bad news follows. Drawing on a two-year study involving journal writing and online interviews of 36 English primary and secondary teachers in 7 primary and 3 secondary schools, *Teacher Professionalism During the Pandemic: Resilience, Courage, Care and Resilience* complicates and repaints part of the picture. Not all news, it turns out, is bad news. In fact, following the initial "extreme turbulence" caused by the pandemic, as reported, many teachers rediscovered "what it means to be a committed professional in challenging times." Speaking for themselves, many of the teachers report developing new skill sets, reemphasizing the place of relationships and relationship building with children and their families as central to the work of teaching, gaining greater appreciation of and respect for their colleagues and school-building administrators so that trust grew; and rediscovering the moral reasons so central to teacher identity that initially led them to becoming teachers. Despite the challenges that came with the pandemic and the herculean effort needed to protect the children and to care for their well-being in dangerous times, the story told is one of human resilience, courage and commitment and as such is inspiring and hopeful.'

Robert V. Bullough, Jr. Emeritus Professor of Teacher Education, Center for the Improvement of Teacher Education and Schooling (CITES), Brigham Young University, USA and Emeritus Professor of Educational Studies, University of Utah, USA

TEACHER PROFESSIONALISM DURING THE PANDEMIC

Courage, Care and Resilience

Christopher Day, Helen Victoria Smith, Ruth Graham and Despoina Athanasiadou

LONDON AND NEW YORK

Cover image: © iStock / Getty Images Plus

First published 2024
by Routledge
4 Park Square, Milton Park, Abingdon, Oxon OX14 4RN

and by Routledge
605 Third Avenue, New York, NY 10158

Routledge is an imprint of the Taylor & Francis Group, an informa business

© 2024 Christopher Day, Helen Victoria Smith, Ruth Graham, Despoina Athanasiadou

The right of Christopher Day, Helen Victoria Smith, Ruth Graham, and Despoina Athanasiadou to be identified as authors of this work has been asserted in accordance with sections 77 and 78 of the Copyright, Designs and Patents Act 1988.

All rights reserved. No part of this book may be reprinted or reproduced or utilised in any form or by any electronic, mechanical, or other means, now known or hereafter invented, including photocopying and recording, or in any information storage or retrieval system, without permission in writing from the publishers.

Trademark notice: Product or corporate names may be trademarks or registered trademarks, and are used only for identification and explanation without intent to infringe.

British Library Cataloguing-in-Publication Data
A catalogue record for this book is available from the British Library

Library of Congress Cataloging-in-Publication Data
Names: Day, Christopher, 1943- author. | Smith, Helen Victoria, 1974- author. | Graham, Ruth (Education assistant professor), author. | Athanasiadou, Despoina, author.
Title: Teacher professionalism during the pandemic : courage, care, and resilience / Christopher Day, Helen Victoria Smith, Ruth Graham, Despoina Athanasiadou.
Description: Abingdon, Oxon ; New York, NY : Routledge, 2024. | Includes bibliographical references and index.
Identifiers: LCCN 2023024758 (print) | LCCN 2023024759 (ebook) | ISBN 9781032489681 (hardback) | ISBN 9781032489674 (paperback) | ISBN 9781003391661 (ebook)
Subjects: LCSH: Teachers--Professional ethics. | COVID-19 Pandemic, 2020- | Teachers--Social conditions. | Teachers--Professional relationships. | Social distancing (Public health) and education.
Classification: LCC LB1779 .D42 2024 (print) | LCC LB1779 (ebook) | DDC 371.1--dc23/eng/20230714
LC record available at https://lccn.loc.gov/2023024758
LC ebook record available at https://lccn.loc.gov/2023024759

ISBN: 978-1-032-48968-1 (hbk)
ISBN: 978-1-032-48967-4 (pbk)
ISBN: 978-1-003-39166-1 (ebk)

DOI: 10.4324/9781003391661

Typeset in Galliard
by Taylor & Francis Books

We thank each one of the 36 primary and secondary teachers whose willingness to share their experiences over a two-year period in the face of unprecedented personal and professional challenges of COVID-19 made this book possible. Their stories serve also as a reminder of the commitment, care, resilience and courage of many millions of teachers across the world, in the service of the learning, welfare and wellbeing of their pupils.

CONTENTS

1	Professionalism in times of change	1
2	Building relationships and managing emotions: Early-career teachers' perspectives	10
3	Adapting to the challenges: Mid-career teachers' perspectives	28
4	Teaching as service: Later-career teachers' perspectives	41
5	Navigating the storm: Occupational and subjective wellbeing	53
6	Professional identities: The importance of agency	69
7	Commitment to care	83
8	Organisational belonging and commitment: The importance of trust	97
9	Teacher professionalism: More than the sum of the parts	108

References	*121*
Appendix 1: Pupils entitled to free school meals (FSM) national averages	*129*
Appendix 2: Interview protocols	*130*
Index	*134*

1

PROFESSIONALISM IN TIMES OF CHANGE

Introduction

This book reports the lived experiences of teachers in primary and secondary schools, who struggled, often experiencing personal and professional challenges to their personal and professional welfare, wellbeing and sense of professional identity and capacity for resilience, and who not only survived the worst threats of the COVID-19 pandemic to their mental and physical health and wellbeing, but did so with their sense of professionalism and commitment to making a positive difference in the learning lives of young people battered but intact, and in some cases strengthened. The book is dedicated to the teachers whose stories made this book possible, but also to those many others in school systems throughout the world like them – whether in their early, mid or late careers, in primary or secondary schools, serving children and young people from rural, urban, advantaged or socio-economically disadvantaged communities – who continue to teach to their best under circumstances and in conditions which are not always supportive to the passion with which they entered teaching.

Throughout the period of the worst ravages of the pandemic, health professionals, care workers and teachers were among the most important frontline workers who continued to provide their services. In England, it is important to remember the days when people emerged briefly but with regularity from their locked down homes to applaud the work of health services. Strangely, they did not do so for the teachers. Yet, marks of workers in both these services were their remarkable capacities for sustaining their professionalism in serving others during a period which tested their resolve as no other had.

The stories which are told in these pages are reflective, sometimes raw with emotion, but always reflecting particular truths at particular times and in particular contexts over a two year period of the COVID-19 pandemic. The

DOI: 10.4324/9781003391661-1

2 Professionalism in times of change

book attempts to capture the authenticity of the professional and the person within. It is written deliberately in a 'readerly' way, respectful of the experiences shared, and informed by a range of research, to appeal to educators in schools, teacher educators in universities. It is written also for all those who, like its authors, care about the education of children and young people in our schools, and who know how important it is that they are taught by teachers who are willing and able to sustain their commitment to their welfare, well-being and academic engagement, progress and achievement.

The book arises from a two-year British Academy/Leverhulme funded research project in which 36 teachers from seven primary and three secondary schools in England agreed to share their ongoing experiences of, and responses to, the pandemic through a series of five online individual interviews and journal writing between September 2020 and September 2022. They worked in schools serving a range of urban and suburban communities. None of the schools was rated as 'outstanding' and none was rated as 'inadequate' by the independent school inspection service in England (Ofsted) (for school details, see Appendix 1). The teachers represent a purposive mix of early, middle and later career experience. Because much of what the teachers shared was sensitive personal and professional data, we have anonymised their names and deliberately de-identified school location and other contextual data. We have also placed the teachers in 'early' (0–7 years teaching experience), 'middle' (8–23 years of teaching experience), and 'later' (23+ years of teaching experience) groupings, rather than their specific number of years teaching, and teaching at the current school, in order to protect their identities. Interviews were semi-structured, conducted using 'Teams' software, at times which suited teachers' needs, transcribed, and thematically analysed (Braun & Clarke, 2006). They focused on: *Year 1 Biography*: professional challenges and responses (Autumn term, 2020); *Return to school following 'lockdown'*: pupil needs and effects on teachers (Spring term, 2021); school support: 'recovery' and 'catch up' learning and teaching pressures; work-life management; commitment (Summer Term, 2021); *Year 2 Professionalism*: teacher identity, resilience, wellbeing; pupil welfare, wellbeing, and academic progress (Autumn 2021); *Change*: effects of pandemic on teacher motivation, commitment, resilience, autonomy; school leadership (Spring, 2022) (see Appendix 2 for details).

Turbulence and perturbations

No one person, local organisation or national system of government in any country, inside or outside education, found it easy to navigate their way through the pandemic. England was no exception. As in other countries,

> Some parents started to withdraw their children from school, teacher absence rose as members of staff took on shielding responsibilities or became fearful for their own vulnerability, long-planned and richly

anticipated school trips planned for the summer and autumn were post-poned, as were parents' evenings and school-based training sessions for school governors; and the teacher union conferences, a long-standing feature of the Easter break, were cancelled.

(Bailey & Breslin, 2021, p. 3)

Many, especially those who were the most vulnerable in societies, were unable to survive the on-going pandemic. Health services in all countries were overwhelmed, education services were compromised and the consequences are still being felt across the world.

Like every teacher in every country in the world over that period, their professionalism was being tested to the limits, as they and their colleagues sought to manage radical changes to their working practices, challenges to their sense of identity as teachers and their commitment to teaching. These changes were caused by the initial shock waves of the pandemic, followed by a series of on-going 'perturbations' which were to continue to challenge the stability of their professional health and welfare, that of their pupils and families and their ability to teach to their best.

The experiences of schools and teachers since the beginning of the pandemic may be characterised as being in two phases. The first might be defined as extreme 'turbulence', in which modes of operation in the environments in which they lived and worked, access to valued resources and relationships with pupils, colleagues, friends and relatives were radically disrupted. Uncertainties increased exponentially about how to maintain personal and professional health, whilst continuing to provide education for all pupils whose welfare and that of their families was threatened, many of whom were unable to engage in face-to-face teaching and learning. The second phase, contiguous with the first, was one of 'perturbance' (Beabout, 2012) as teachers entered a period of learning to develop and implement ways of managing the new environment. Individual and organisational practices were adjusted to bring order to turbulence, to mediate its initial effects and to manage the new teaching and learning environments, even as perturbations continued.

A report of the work of school trusts in four regions of England (groups of schools under the leadership of trustees) detailed the multitude of activities in which school leaders and teachers engaged over the period. That these were able to be managed is impressive by any standards:

- Re-distributing responsibilities among staff
- Re-framing policies and practices for health and safety
- Building and sustaining school-wide collegiality
- Innovations in teaching and learning: the development and enhancement of technology
- Engaging pupils in remote learning
- Minimising disengagement, especially of vulnerable pupils and families

4 Professionalism in times of change

- Connecting with others
- Optimising communication with families
- Ensuring pupils' welfare and wellbeing
- Monitoring pupils' learning engagement and evaluating progress
- Supporting staff morale and wellbeing
- Sustaining a broad curriculum

(Day et al., 2021)

It is worth briefly reminding readers of the patterns of disruption at system level in England during this period in which the research took place, and to which schools and teachers responded. They are charted here as 'milestones'. The first milestone (*Milestone 1*) refers to the first national lockdown in March 2020, when attendance was restricted to vulnerable pupils and the children of key workers, and schools moved rapidly to providing remote education for all other pupils. *Milestone 2* is associated with the wider re-opening of schools (beginning with primary schools) with strict public health controls in place in June 2020, and processes for school- based test and examination grades initiated. *Milestone 3* (in September 2020), signalled a full return to schooling for all pupils. However, in some areas, rolling closures of 'bubbles' (when one or more pupils in a class contracted the virus, that class was sent home) resulted in significant disruption in some schools. In November 2020 (*Milestone 4*), there was a second national lockdown. Schools were required to remain open despite significant disruption in some areas due to staff and pupil absence. *Milestone 5* (January 2021) refers to the starting up of COVID-19 testing on secondary school sites and the beginning of the third national lockdown. Once again, attendance to schools was restricted to vulnerable pupils and the children of key workers. All other pupils were educated remotely until *Milestone 6*, the beginning of March 2021, when schools were re-opened for all pupils (Day, Taneva & Smith, 2021). The research began in the Autumn term of 2020 (*Milestone 3*), and so the teachers' responses in the first interviews were informed by their experiences of the previous six-month period. Others (interviews 2–5) coincided with *Milestones 4, 5,* and *6*.

Throughout these milestones, the extent of the development of efficient, effective means of continuing to educate off-site pupils varied across teachers and schools, as did the academic progression of all pupils. As other research has noted,

> Some schools and teachers were more adept at providing appropriate work, some young people lacked the equipment to access the virtual provision, whatever its quality,…some equipment faltered at either end of the home–school connection – sometimes because of a failure to understand how to use it, rather than a fault with the equipment itself – some battled with limited and crowded home spaces and others battled with the balance between working from home and supporting the learning of their child or children.

(Breslin, 2022, p. 11)

However, the gaps in the academic progression between pupils who did and did not receive free school meals (a proxy for educational disadvantage) grew.

Experiencing the turbulence: changing practices, excessive workload, threats to morale and isolation

The recent literature in relation to the pandemic has largely highlighted its negative effects on teachers' workload during those testing times – the stresses, the disenchantment, the threats to morale and mental health, the lack of timely government support and, as a consequence, increased intentions to leave the profession. An Education Policy Institute survey of teachers in English schools, for example, found that intentions to leave had increased significantly after two years of the pandemic, and that the main reason was dissatisfaction with the government's management – what were described as poor, 'reckless,' and 'irresponsible' decisions taken by governments (Breslin, 2022; Fullard, 2021; Ridley, 2020).

Surveys by national teachers' organisations have found adverse effects of work-related stress, with over half their members reporting that their workload was unmanageable, 44% intending to leave teaching by 2027 (National Education Union, 2022), and 84% saying that their job had adversely affected their mental health (National Association of School-masters Union of Women Teachers, 2022). A survey commissioned by the National Association of Head Teachers/Association of School and College Leaders also found negative results reported by school leaders:

> Significant proportions of leaders in all types of schools and in all demographic groups have struggled with work-related stress, workload and change fatigue during the pandemic. Two thirds (65%) report that they have been 'mostly surviving' (42%) or 'sometimes/mostly sinking' (23%).
>
> *(Thomson et al., 2021)*

These and other studies have been valuable in charting the negative effects of the pandemic on teachers' physical and emotional energy, mental health and the dimming of their desire to remain in the profession. However, many have been conducted retrospectively, through snapshot surveys and interviews. Few studies have taken a deep dive into teachers' responses to the changed and changing work conditions, and continuing challenges to health and welfare as they were experienced over time.

Our research findings mirrored the evidence of work-related stress, workload, dissatisfaction with government expressed by others, but teachers interviewed in this research expressed no intentions to leave as a result of the pandemic. In contrast, our research found, over the two-year period, more nuanced, more hopeful perspectives reported to us by the participants.

6 Professionalism in times of change

We do not assume that these are generalisable across the profession, nor do we suggest that these teachers were more, or less effective than others in their work and in what their pupils achieved. However, the courage, conviction, care, resilience and commitment that they reported over the two years of the research do suggest that there is an alternative, more hopeful view of teachers that does not present them as passive victims of circumstances which they are unable to manage. It is this which they reported, and which is the primary focus of this book.

We do not claim that other narratives, in which disenchantment and alienation dominate, are false in the ways that they represent the huge challenges faced by all, as a result of the dramatically changed contexts in which teachers worked and students learned. On the contrary, it is important at the outset that these reports are acknowledged. Indeed, teachers in the project spoke of the same challenges during their interview responses, and through their written journals.

> My morale this term has been very low. I've found it difficult to adjust to online learning. The government had high expectations and I found it difficult to keep up with the workload. Although I would consider myself a confident user of technology, I did not find it easy. My resilience levels were low. I always strive to provide the best education for the children in my care but due to the short notice about schools not returning after the Christmas holiday. I found it difficult to provide high quality online learning at such short notice.
>
> *(Lucy, primary, early, Journal 2)*

My school life is miserable in comparison to what I was used to. I am a social person. I like my friends at my job, and I love the companionship within a team. However, due to the nature of 'bubble' rules, we don't have this as much. As time went on, we went to virtual staff meetings, which work but are not the same as having face-to-face conversations.

Most days I work from 8am-6pm, I feel like I should be able to do my job, and do it well, within those hours, but I can't. I made a list of everything I can think of that I have to fit in throughout the year, the things that affect my work-life balance and stress levels. I know there's lots more, but these are the regulars:

- 3 x weekly meetings (whole-school, morning meet, phase meet)
- after-school clubs (not optional)
- 2/3 break duties weekly
- weekly recorded observations (union guidance states that it should be one a term)
- 150 bubble and blocks weekly (marking policy)
- assessing every single topic every half-term

Professionalism in times of change **7**

> - subject lead duties which no extra pay is given for (long term plans for whole school, supporting documents, meetings, book looks)
> - 15 pages of planning weekly
> - filling out behaviour-tracking documents
> - no PPA on weeks before holidays
>
> *(Cate, primary, early, Journal 5)*

Two teachers who were clinically vulnerable spoke of their sense of isolation from their professional colleagues. Emma, a primary teacher whose poor health meant that she was absent from school for extended periods, felt that the school was 'dismissive' of her concerns about catching COVID-19.

> 'It feels like I am being punished. It's frowned upon to be off sick...I remember putting something in an email like, "I really feel isolated; I feel a bit lost." I feel ignored'.
>
> *(Emma, primary, middle, Interview 1)*

Mark, an experienced secondary teacher, spoke of his sense of being 'different', even when all pupils returned to schools. Due to his clinically vulnerable status, he had to enforce mask wearing in his classroom, as he was fearful for his health.

> You can't have a teacher that isn't confident in a classroom, you need to be confident. The old teacher in me subconsciously sometimes might wander over to a child that wants to ask a question, but I've quickly got to draw myself back and constantly put a screen between myself and the children. The children don't like it, I don't like it, but it's an absolute must... I think it's very stressful if we're at the front end, whether it be in teaching or the medical profession or the caring profession, it's very stressful.
>
> *(Mark, secondary, middle, Interview 4)*

Others experienced at least a temporary drop in their morale as a result of difficulties in adjusting to online learning, and untimely communication of government decisions with regard to school openings for all pupils.

The evidence that was accrued from the participants in the project confirms that this period represented previously unexperienced academic, practical and wellbeing challenges. However, almost all the teachers who shared their experiences over this two-year period provided different, more positive responses to the challenges. All but two had no intention of leaving the profession, often citing their ongoing commitment to the pupils, relationships with colleagues, schools and their communities as positive factors in their journey through the difficulties. These teachers experienced the same tumult, disruptions, perturbations and discontinuities to lives and livelihoods that pervade much of the recent research, but their responses present a more

8 Professionalism in times of change

nuanced picture of teacher professionalism. *They provide counter-narratives to the stories of initial and ongoing distress reported above.*

The overwhelming number did not characterise themselves as 'victims' of circumstance, poor leadership or unhelpful school cultures and national policies, though, as we will see, all figured in their responses. On the contrary, despite these, they demonstrated their commitment, belief that they were continuing to make a difference in the learning lives and welfare of their pupils, persistence of care, resilience, a strong sense of identity and dedication and hope for the future. Arguably, together with the possession of knowledge and skills appropriate to their work, these are fundamental parts of what teacher professionalism means. *We believe that they deserve to be heard and read, not only in themselves, but also because they demonstrate what it means to be a committed professional in challenging times.*

In early interviews, Teresa commented that engaging the pupils in the new online teaching that she and her colleagues had spent a long-time planning had been 'very disheartening'.

> You realise that out of the 20 children that you want to access this lesson, only seven of them did. It was the motivation that became hard because we're doing the very best we can, but not all the children could access it. And sometimes it got frustrating.
>
> *(Teresa, primary, middle, Interview 2)*

However, her care for the children and their families shone through as she recalled preparing food packages for parents who were struggling, and offering school places to families that needed them.

Dawn also spoke of an intensification of workload in preparing online learning materials.

> I've never really known this before – lots of preparation because we're having to prepare so much with different children at different levels. Workload's been very high. But I'm not bothered. It's not affected be in any negative way, really, other than being tired. The workload just seems to be intensifying.
>
> *(Dawn, primary, later, Interview 3)*

Responses from these two experienced teachers were widely shared by early and later career colleagues in both primary and secondary schools.

Mia missed the human interaction with her colleagues and pupils.

> I think teaching is one of those jobs you go into because you love that interaction and being with people – and it's not the same when it's on the computer over the internet.... being online showed me how much I want to be in the classroom...So for me, it's helped to reaffirm that I am in the right job.
>
> *(Mia, secondary, early, Interview 2)*

Gina, a senior secondary school teacher, did not think that the increases in workload had made people less likely to want to stay in teaching, and that the pandemic had, 'brought to the forefront how important teaching is, rather than the opposite...people feel very proud of what they've achieved' (Interview 2).

She was frustrated with the government's changes to the criteria for the 'risk assessment' of pupils as they returned to school, but 'proud' of the way she and her colleagues across the school were 'doing everything we can to make things work and how we kept doing that all the way through', though it had been 'hard', and spoke of her ongoing commitment to her job and the importance of care in the face of difficulties.

Though there is little doubt that teachers' physical, intellectual and mental resolve were tested to their limits as they responded to continuing, often unpredictable, changes over which they had little control, at least initially, as they sought to manage the unexpected turbulence and continuing perturbations, all demonstrated their 'professionalism', a word often used but not always well-defined.

Conclusions

It is often forgotten that throughout the many restrictions, schools remained open for the children of frontline workers and the vulnerable. Teachers themselves, under the guidance of their leaders, developed and supported online technologies to provide home learning for others, whilst also providing support for the welfare needs of families in challenging socio-economic circumstances through, for example, the provision and often personal delivery of food parcels. It is difficult to over-estimate the importance of their civic roles, especially those who taught pupils from highly disadvantaged communities, in supporting parents and families in their local communities. The different responses of the teachers speak directly and indirectly to their commitment, care, resilience, continuing optimism and hope. The evidence from our research project confirms this, and highlights their courage in continuing to strive to teach to their best, despite the challenging and changing circumstances. This book is for teachers who, like many around the world, 'have good days and bad, and whose bad days bring the suffering that comes only from something we love. It is for teachers who refuse to harden their hearts because they love learners, learning, and the teaching life' (Palmer, 1998, p. 1). It also reveals that while courage is undoubtedly an essential characteristic of any teaching, as the management of turbulence and perturbances in the chapters in the book will reveal, it is only one of the variables that illustrate the capacities and capabilities on which these teachers drew as they continued their work over this most challenging period.

2

BUILDING RELATIONSHIPS AND MANAGING EMOTIONS

Early-career teachers' perspectives

Introduction

Previous research (Day, 2008; Gu & Day, 2007) has shown that whilst teachers in the early phase of their career (0–3 years) are highly committed to work, they require support from colleagues and school leaders in order to develop their sense of efficacy, especially if dealing with poor pupil behaviour. As teachers enter years four to seven of teaching, they are able to gain greater confidence in their effectiveness, particularly if given additional responsibilities. Moreover, if able to build a sense of self-efficacy through positive experiences and opportunities, these teachers can persist in times of turbulence and change (Gu & Day, 2007). In addition, early-phase teachers, once they have learned to manage the emotional labour of teaching, are often more able to adapt to change due to growing up in a more uncertain, insecure world and not having had the time to become set in their ways like longer-serving teachers (Hargreaves, 2005).

This chapter reveals how 12 teachers who had been qualified for less than seven years at the start of the study experienced the different challenges they faced during the pandemic, and the impact of these on their commitment to their work. The chapter begins by describing how they reflected on their role as they built connections with their pupils and, in doing so, recognised the importance of the pupil-teacher relationship and its association with their sense of purpose and desire to do their best. It then considers how changes in the teaching and learning contexts caused fluctuations in their sense of self-efficacy which, in turn, impacted their emotional wellbeing and motivation. Finally, the chapter examines the impact of colleagues and leaders on early career teachers' wellbeing, resilience, sense of professionalism and commitment to teaching as a long-term career.

DOI: 10.4324/9781003391661-2

The meaning of teaching: care as a key purpose

> I think it was the first time that I realised that being a teacher is not just about teaching content and getting the kids to pass exams to get to where they want to be. It's actually about looking out for them.
>
> *(Kath, secondary, Interview 1)*

Teaching is both an intellectual and an emotional practice (Denzin, 1984; Hargreaves, 2000, O'Connor, 2008). As discussed more fully in Chapter 7, at its best, it involves both caring about and for pupils. We can understand caring *about* pupils as the concern a teacher feels for them but does not act on, whereas caring *for* pupils involves paying attention, building a relationship and developing empathy, which results in deliberate, purposeful action (Gay, 2018; Noddings, 2013). During the two-year period of the research, early-phase teachers spoke about noticing pupils with greater social and emotional needs and the importance of caring *for* pupils who had experienced bereavement, isolation from family and friends and difficult home circumstances. These teachers did not just care *about* their pupils; they also invested a considerable amount of emotional work to care *for* them.

Five out of the six early-phase secondary teachers found themselves shifting their focus from teaching their subject and emphasis on academic progress and attainment, to placing more emphasis on supporting pupils' social and emotional wellbeing. Anna, a first-year secondary teacher and form tutor, was worried about the trauma that the pandemic had inflicted on some of her pupils.

> Our focus has shifted to asking the question, 'Is what we do actually going to help, to benefit them? Am I able to make this an enjoyable part of their life?' So, the focus has shifted a little more to relationships rather than what grades they will get.
>
> *(Anna, secondary, Interview 1)*

As the pandemic continued, Anna became increasingly concerned about the impact of it on pupils' mental health as she found 'in all of my classes I've got kids that are struggling, really struggling' (Anna, Interview 2). Consequently, her 'job has got more complex because that's a whole new level of emotional work that we have had to do' (Anna, Interview 2). Part of this emotional work was building supportive relationships with her pupils. As a form tutor, Anna described having developed a close relationship with her form and caring deeply about their present and future wellbeing – 'I've just bonded with them in such a phenomenal way, and I could get emotional talking about it' (Anna, Interview 2). Her emotional concerns were also heightened by what she saw as a lack of recognition from the government for the long-term impact of the pandemic on pupils' mental health. She felt that she had to compensate for the government's lack of care by offering care herself.

12 Building relationships, managing emotions

Similarly, as the pandemic continued, other early-phase secondary teachers, such as Patricia, Kath and Max, began to understand their role differently, noting that caring for pupils' wellbeing and safety had become their main focus.

> A lot has come to light with who the vulnerable children are and what their needs are… and the things that they need from teachers rather than just teaching them what they need for passing exams … just empathy for the different situations that children are in, and understanding that they are still children, no matter how annoying they might be in lesson – they are still children.
>
> *(Kath, secondary, Interview 4)*

Having to manage this level of emotional work might have deterred some teachers from staying in the profession, but for these early-phase secondary teachers, their extended care roles gave them a strong sense of purpose. Anna and Max commented on their relationships with pupils as being a strong force in motivating them to stay in the profession. In his journal, Max, a teacher for four years, detailed his concerns about the impact of the pandemic on individual pupils, which he found simultaneously upsetting and motivating.

> One extremely conscientious and polite pupil in my year group lost his Grandad to Covid-19. The Grandad was diagnosed and taken into hospital on the Thursday, and he died on the Sunday. I found this particularly moving and set up some bereavement counselling for the child. I was even more moved when I spoke to the student who responded very maturely and was determined not to let his loss affect his continued efforts online. This made me feel proud to be their… teacher.
>
> *(Max, secondary, Journal 2)*

Max reported that workload pressure and the government's apparent lack of concern for teachers had initially made him think 'about an alternative within education' (Interview 1) but building stronger bonds with his pupils and their families had renewed his commitment to staying in the profession. Similarly, by her third interview, after witnessing many pupils struggling with their wellbeing, Anna was determined to advocate for the professional mental health support she believed was needed in schools.

Being more aware of pupils' struggles and caring for them also highlighted to these teachers the reciprocal nature of teacher-pupil relationships. For Mia, in her second year of secondary teaching, relationships with pupils supported her to stay motivated and committed during this stressful time – 'the students themselves, a lot of the time, are what keep me going' (Interview 4). Furthermore, the ability to build positive relationships with her pupils became key to how Mia viewed her role as a teacher.

Ultimately, you're a role model... we're not just teaching them, we're showing them how they should behave and how they relate to people, and how to go out into the world and be good citizens... There's a lot more to it that just standing in a classroom and teaching them your subject... The ability to build relationships with students. It all comes back to that for me... Showing the students that we're here for them and that we want them to do well. It's not just a job in a lot of ways.

(Mia, secondary, Interview 4)

In the case of the early-phase primary teachers, three out of six talked about how their relationships with pupils underpinned their commitment to teaching. For example, Cate had planned to leave her current job after six years of teaching, but her relationships with pupils helped her to keep going at the start of the pandemic and to stay committed until the end of the year when all schools were once again permanently open to all pupils.

I want to put my full effort in, making sure that these children that are in my care have a brilliant final year of their primary school, so I want to see them out in July. I won't be looking for jobs before then.

(Cate, primary, Interview 4)

Putting pupils first also helped Nina, a third-year primary teacher, to stay committed. She commented that 'I still feel really committed and I want to do well by the children. I still want to put my all in' (Interview 3). Lucy, a fourth-year primary teacher, described missing being with her pupils when they were learning from home (Interview 2) and thinking about her pupils 'before I think about myself most of the time' (Interview 3). She explained,

I think that when you do this job and when you're stood in front of those children and when you have them coming to you every day... you are endlessly committed. And I think that it would take a real lot for me to go 'I'm not committed to them anymore'.

(Lucy, primary, Interview 3)

It seems that teaching in the pandemic helped both primary and secondary early-phase teachers to quickly recognise and value caring, reciprocal relationships with their pupils which, for most, gave them a sense of purpose that supported their motivation and commitment.

Moving on from how these teachers felt about their pupils, the next section examines factors that influenced how they felt about themselves as effective professionals.

Fluctuating self-efficacy

As we will detail in Chapter 5, subjective wellbeing incorporates three key elements – how satisfied people are with their life or aspects of it; people's negative and positive emotional response to their experiences; and people's sense of purpose and competence (Song et al., 2020). That and other research has shown that, for teachers, their confidence in their perceived effectiveness and achievement (self-efficacy) influences their subjective wellbeing. For early-phase teachers particularly, self-efficacy is key to their job satisfaction and commitment to staying in the profession (Moore Johnson, 2004). Furthermore, self-efficacy is an important factor in building resilience (Gu & Li, 2013), and can be positively and negatively influenced by feedback from parents, colleagues and pupils (Day et al, 2007; Day & Gu, 2010). We found that most (ten) of the early-phase teachers in our study experienced fluctuating levels of self-efficacy in response to the various challenges that teaching in a pandemic posed, which affected their subjective wellbeing.

Self-doubt and powerlessness: letting pupils down?

Managing an increasingly complex and emotionally demanding role with more limited contact with colleagues sometimes led primary and secondary early-phase teachers to doubt their abilities and to feel powerless. One reason for this was that usual school procedures for managing challenging pupil behaviour could not be followed due to COVID-19 restrictions (e.g., pupils and teachers being allocated to small groups or 'bubbles' to limit the spread of the virus). Anna discovered that

> behaviour issues were more challenging to deal with because normal procedures, such as detentions in break times or standing in the corridor could not happen due to everyone having to stay in their own 'bubble'.
> *(Anna, secondary, early, Interview 2)*

Mia found that 'some days are quite difficult in terms of behaviour' (Interview 1) and detailed in her journal how one particularly challenging incident with a pupil had resulted in them being excluded and Mia feeling she had let the pupil down, which damaged her self-efficacy. Cate initially blamed lockdowns for increasing incidents of low-level disruption and poor behaviour, having previously felt confident in her ability to build positive relationships and manage pupils' behaviour.

> Previous to this year, I'd say behaviour management has always been a strong point of mine. It comes easy once you've developed positive relationships rooted in mutual respect. On the whole, of course, it is a pleasure to spend time with the children, but if I think about it, many low-level

behaviours are happening throughout the day: constant talking over teaching; verbal and physical playground disputes; and general rudeness to staff. As I did not experience this with last year's Year 6, I am left wondering if the lockdowns have affected these children much more, perhaps because of the developmental stage they were at when it all began.

(Cate, primary, early, Journal 5)

However, Cate's self-efficacy began to be threatened when faced with trying to manage the extreme behaviour of one pupil in her class.

I wasn't managing very well. I felt like I was letting down 90% of children in my class because they'd come out of their lesson having not learned from that lesson because they'd been unable to concentrate due to things happening around them. I feel like I didn't manage that very well, but I don't know what else I could have done... I feel that I perhaps gave in when I shouldn't.

(Cate, primary, early, Interview 4)

A feeling of powerlessness was also reported by Mia and Zoe when unable to answer pupils' questions about the pandemic: 'They come to us to fix things, but we can't do that at the moment' and 'they just don't understand, and they've got so many questions, and we can't always answer them.' (Mia, secondary, Interview 1); 'These kids, they're scared. A lot of them keep telling me, '"We've got vulnerable people at home, why am I at school?" And I don't have an answer for them, and that's the hardest thing' (Zoe, secondary, Interview 1).

Five primary and secondary early-phase teachers reported persistent feelings of self-doubt which were exacerbated by feeling underprepared and having to work in new and unexpected ways. Zoe, a secondary teacher, described constantly battling with self-doubt and Patricia, another secondary teacher, worried about whether she was meeting the needs of all her pupils, particularly the quieter ones who she was no longer able to interact with on an individual basis (due to having to stay at the front of the class). This knocked her confidence. And despite considering herself a competent user of technology, Nina 'found it difficult to provide high quality online learning at such short notice' (Journal 2). As a relatively new primary teacher who was still developing at the same time as feeling a huge responsibility for her pupils' attainment, Nina commented that she had struggled with her resilience. 'There were just such high expectations. Always new things to learn and very little time to learn those things or to get used to it' (Interview 2). Similarly, Gemma, another primary teacher, described feeling

a bit lost in the ocean. I don't feel confident that I know what I'm doing. I'm confident in teaching if the children were in front of me, but posting

16 Building relationships, managing emotions

it online is very strange. I don't know if the children are getting out of it what they should.

(Interview 1)

And another primary teacher, Cate, worried about her video-recorded lessons being judged badly by colleagues, pupils and parents, resulting in a greater workload as she spent hours trying to perfect them.

> I found myself more conscious of my appearance for the videos and even when I tried to record them all in a chunk on Saturdays, it was taking me hours because any little slip-up and I was restarting, terrified of being judged by anyone who saw.
>
> *(Cate, primary, Journal 2)*

Three early-phase teachers complained about a lack of time and opportunities for professional learning and collaboration. Moore Johnson's (2004) long-itudinal study of fifty early career teachers in the USA demonstrated that teachers who are provided with regular space and time to gain constructive feedback from more experienced colleagues and share ideas, are more likely to experience success and, subsequently, a greater sense of self-efficacy. This was the case for Mia, who initially lost confidence when struggling to manage poor pupil behaviour due to COVID-19 restrictions, but through the support of colleagues who related similar challenges, was able to boost her sense of self-efficacy and find a way forward.

> This has made me re-evaluate how I can continue to adapt our behaviour techniques to the current situation. Having discussed this incident with colleagues I found others feel the same way and it has enabled us to support each other to come up with new ideas.
>
> *(Mia, secondary, Journal 2)*

However, Mia also commented that she would have liked opportunities to observe more experienced colleagues but was unable to due to COVID-19 restrictions – 'it's difficult because, normally, I need to go and observe another member of staff or go have a meeting with someone to share ideas and that sort of thing' (Interview 1). Similarly, Patricia, who was already worried about the learning opportunities she had missed whilst training to be a teacher at the start of the pandemic, found she could not collaborate and learn from teachers in different departments due to being confined to working with her department colleagues only. Lucy also struggled with the limited contact she had with colleagues due to being restricted by the requirement for 'bubbles' (groups of pupils and staff that could only mix with each other). Like Mia, Lucy wanted to be able to observe, and be observed by, more experienced colleagues so she could be assured in, and develop, her practice. And like Patricia, Lucy's professional development was reduced to virtual meetings with few opportunities for professional dialogue or collaboration with colleagues. Teaching in the pandemic therefore meant reduced opportunities for professional development and positive feedback, making it more difficult for these early-phase teachers to develop their practice and self-efficacy through gaining the reassurance and guidance of more experienced colleagues.

Ensuring pupils were learning, whether at home or in school, was another reason for self-doubt. Anna explained that working incredibly hard but feeling that she was not impacting her pupils' learning had caused her to nearly burn out. However, instead of giving up, she had stepped back and re-evaluated her practice.

> I was trying to force through the subject before the curiosity… Teaching from a place of love, teaching from a place of nurture and authenticity has enabled me to … have more success… That's what's been exciting for me about this year.
>
> *(Anna, secondary, Interview 2)*

In Anna's case, self-doubt and near burnout led to self-reflection and adapting her practice which, in turn, enhanced her sense of self-efficacy and resilience. These were further reinforced by positive feedback from colleagues and pupils.

> Currently I feel really proud … That I've got here. I'm still here … I made it through my NQT [newly qualified teacher] year, and I've got great feedback from people, and I've got a fantastic department, and I've made some progress with some kids, and I've got kids that like me and respect me and that is an achievement.
>
> *(Anna, secondary, Interview 3)*

Letting parents down?

However, negative feedback from parents meant Anna's sense of self-efficacy fluctuated, highlighting the emotional nature of her work.

> When you get an email from a parent saying, 'why has my daughter dropped three grades in one year, can you explain that?' and you can't reply with a one-word email that just says 'COVID?' Maybe that's the reason. I don't know. Then you have to put on the professional voice and then you get another email, another email and another email and I question myself. I question my own judgement… 'Is it me? Am I doing a good enough job?' 'I'm doing a good enough job'. That is the whole cycle of emotions of being a teacher, I think. It's the 'I'm doing okay, I'm doing enough' and 'I'm not doing okay and I'm not doing enough' and you just go round and round and round until you level out somewhere, hopefully.
>
> *(Anna, secondary, Interview 3)*

18 Building relationships, managing emotions

Feedback from parents impacted other early-phase teachers' confidence and sense of self-efficacy too. Criticism from her pupils' parents led to Lucy losing confidence in her abilities.

> Being verbally abused by stressed-out parents and their expectations on me. I was doing as much as I could and more. It made me feel like no amount of support that I had provided was good enough.
>
> *(Lucy, primary, Journal 2)*

For Cate too, a negative interaction with a parent, who accused her of not doing enough, left her feeling demoralised and demotivated even though she knew she was doing her best during a very challenging time.

> I felt completely unappreciated and immediately began to question why I bother, as the things that I go out of my way to do never get noticed, just the things that people don't like and are often out of my control anyway. I can't stop thinking about the fact that I am probably perceived by most people as 'having it easy'. This was the last interaction I had before the Easter holidays, and it left my motivation at a real low.
>
> *(Cate, primary, Journal 2)*

In contrast, praise from parents gave Nina a greater sense of self-efficacy which enhanced her motivation.

> I received some positive messages from parents thanking me and the school for all we were doing. One parent said that, as a working parent who was working from home, she appreciated the balance that the school and myself were providing. She complemented the activities and support we were providing. This made me feel motivated to continue to provide the best learning for the children.
>
> *(Nina, primary, Journal 2)*

Although Anna's self-efficacy fluctuated, she came to accept that teaching was an emotional endeavour and, by recognising her achievements and resilience, she was able to maintain her self-efficacy. She described feeling proud of what she had accomplished during a particularly challenging time.

> There's definitely a pride in what I've achieved this year and what I've just done to get through it … I didn't quit, and no one got badly hurt and I did my job and I taught some really good lessons. And here we are a year later, still going.
>
> *(Anna, secondary, Interview 4)*

Navigating the many challenges of teaching during a pandemic also gave Patricia and Kath confidence in their abilities and optimism that teaching would become easier.

> If I've managed to do that, then carrying on teaching has got to be a breeze – it's going to get easier… So, if anything, it's probably just made me realise that actually I can do it.
>
> *(Patricia, secondary, Interview 2)*

> Going forward, I know that there's going to be, there's light at the end of the tunnel. It's not always going to be like this. I know I've managed this far, so there's no reason why I can't continue.
>
> *(Kath, secondary, Interview 3)*

Although the majority of early-phase teachers experienced feelings of self-doubt and powerlessness due to interrupted training years, a lack of professional development opportunities, new and unexpected ways of working, challenging pupil behaviour and negative parent feedback, overcoming these challenges and gaining positive feedback was important for enhancing their sense of achievement and self-efficacy. As a result, they were able to build resilience, sustain commitment to their work (Keogh et al., 2012, cited in Song et al., 2020) and even feel optimistic about the future.

Having examined how early-phase teachers felt about themselves as professionals, the next section reveals how they felt about their colleagues and leaders.

Relationships with colleagues and leaders

As the first section of this chapter showed, developing caring, reciprocal relationships with pupils was important to both primary and secondary early-phase teachers, giving them a sense of purpose, commitment, and motivation. This section reveals how their relationships with colleagues and school leaders also played a significant role in how they experienced and understood their work.

Supporting and supportive colleagues

Supportive relationships with colleagues are important for teachers' commitment, resilience, and effectiveness (Day et al., 2005; Gu & Day, 2013).

> We're all experiencing the same challenges, similar challenges… it's like you come together, don't you? Isn't that natural when you are going through a rocky time together?
>
> *(Cate, primary, Interview 4)*

20 Building relationships, managing emotions

Seven early-phase teachers placed great value on their relationships with the colleagues they worked most closely with. Max appreciated having a colleague who provided mutual support at a time when work was 'incredibly demanding' (Interview 2). 'I work very closely with somebody at work, and we bounce a lot of ideas off each other. We try and share with each other a positive from the day and try and focus on that' (Interview 2). Having her colleagues' support was also important to Patricia. 'If ever there's been any concerns… somebody reassured you or they found out the information for you… In terms of that, it's been absolutely fantastic' (Interview 1) and 'the department remains extremely close and supportive, with my mentor and other staff continuously checking in with each other, to see how we are all getting on' (Journal 1). Throughout her interviews and journal entries, Mia valued being in a supportive school where she felt they were 'all in it together' (Interview 1). She viewed her colleagues as her 'family' (Interview 2), felt 'massively supported' (Interview 2) and appreciated 'a sense of pulling together and rallying' (Interview 4). Similarly, Anna reported being 'in an incredible department with an incredible staff. We are constantly sharing lesson plans, share the load in marking' (Interview 1), and Kath felt well supported by a sense of community where everybody wanted to help each other. Like Mia, Anna saw her colleagues as her family and friends. She felt that everyone was 'pulling together and doing their best' (Interview 1) and that 'they have looked after me in ways that they probably won't ever realise. It's been an incredibly affirming experience to be with these people' (Interview 2). Cate also held her colleagues in high regard. 'We have a strong collegial culture… we share resources. My partners pull their weight, we trust each other' (Interview 1) and 'my year group partner is brilliant this year… My TA that we share… he's amazing too. I have an amazing team' (Interview 4). Cate's year group team had also set up an online chat forum which supported Cate's resilience.

> We share anecdotes and whether our morale is high or low doesn't matter – misery loves company and having them there to chat to is uplifting! I am lucky to be in the team that I am. My resilience is much stronger knowing that they are there to sympathise, relate to and support me, as I am them.
>
> *(Cate, primary, Journal 2)*

For Zoe, it was her relationships with colleagues that had helped her keep going.

> We've all kind of stuck together and had each other's back and tried to support one another. I think that's one of the things that's got me through, is having that network there.
>
> *(Zoe, secondary, Interview 1)*

Building relationships, managing emotions   21

It seems that collegiality and connection with other teachers who were having similar experiences gave these teachers relational resilience which helped them to stay committed and cope with the various challenges they faced (Day & Gu, 2010).

Being let down by school leaders

School leadership matters in sustaining a sense of resilience, commitment, and effectiveness among the staff. Building resilience in an organisational setting places a great deal of importance on the effectiveness of the orga-nisational context, structure and system, and on how the system functions as a whole to create a supportive environment for individuals' profes-sional learning and development, to build a trusting relationship amongst its staff, to foster a collective sense of efficacy and resilience and, through this, to sustain its continuous improvement.

(Gu & Day, 2013, p. 38)

In contrast to how they felt about their close colleagues, four (two primary and two secondary) early-phase teachers were disappointed by the actions of some school leaders. For example, Lucy felt senior leaders had lost sight of what it was like to be a class teacher, had made decisions without considering the negative impact they would have on teachers, and were not receptive to teachers who were struggling. One of Cate's reasons for planning to leave her job was that she felt let down by senior leaders who did not offer support when she asked for help to manage a pupil's challenging behaviour. She had resorted to turning desperately to anyone that would listen.

I've admitted it to everyone and anyone who listened, not just leadership. I've said to the dinner ladies for example, or my TA [teaching assistant] or my year group partner. I've said to everybody, 'I don't know what to do, so if you have any suggestions, help me.

(Cate, primary, Interview 4)

Cate needed to receive strong support from leaders. As Day and Gu reported,

although disruptive pupil behaviour may have a detrimental effect upon new teachers' abilities and willingness to sustain their commitment, where there were strong leadership support and responsive professional devel-opment opportunities, many were able to build upon their initial sense of vocation and resilience.

(Day & Gu, 2010, p. 68)

Anna was frustrated by a senior leadership team whom she felt had not given teachers time to prepare for schools fully reopening after the first lockdown. 'I felt very much like I was a cog in a machine in that first week back, because we were thrown into it straightaway' (Interview 1). She blamed senior leaders for creating extra workload and pressure through their timing of assessments, changes to timetables and quick decisions. 'They threw a lot at us' (Interview 2) and 'I think it was already hard. It was already a tough year. It was already challenging... The workload has just been insane' (Interview 3). Anna pleaded for senior leaders to 'leave us alone now. Leave us alone. We've worked really hard, say "thank you", say "thank you". That's all we want' (Interview 3). And her frustration with senior leaders' decisions continued when she described them implementing a 'deep dive' with only one week's notice, causing a lot of stress and upset in her department as teachers were already busy with marking assessments, inputting data, parents' evenings and report writing. Anna told one of the leaders,

> I'm disappointed. I think it's a real shame that you've done this. I think it's been badly explained. The timing of it is bizarre. And I'm sure you've got reasons in SLT [senior leadership team] land, but you haven't communicated them to us.
>
> *(Anna, secondary, Interview 4)*

Managing workload and wellbeing

Increased workloads and poor mental health were experienced by many teachers during the pandemic (NASUWT, 2022) including seven of the early-phase teachers in our study. Like Anna, teachers commented on the negative impact of excessive workloads on their personal lives and wellbeing. By her second interview, Nina was feeling overwhelmed. 'I feel like I'm working all the time' (Interview 2) and, in the following term, she felt her mental health was declining due to being 'so busy and stressed at work' (Interview 3). Max described 'feeling mentally quite strained and quite exhausted' (Interview 1) and work being 'incredibly demanding' (Interview 2), leading him to question whether he wanted to relinquish an extra responsibility he had been given so he could reduce his workload. Mia also depicted the amount of work as 'really overwhelming' (Interview 1) and was 'working a lot more at the weekends than I normally would.' (Interview 3). Anna repeatedly referred to feeling fed up and exhausted, with staff morale and mental health being at the lowest she had seen. 'We've had enough... it's been a lot from all angles' (Interview 3) and 'We're living in this constant hamster wheel of making decisions on the fly, planning, not having enough time, not having enough time' (Interview 3). Feeling tired due to working long hours had made Isla, a primary teacher, question whether teaching would be a long-term career. 'I just think if I'm going to have my own children and have any time to unwind, I can't see myself teaching over the age of forty' (Interview 1).

By her third interview, Lucy felt 'mentally, physically just drained' and was worried about her ability to keep going. 'I have not stopped once. We had to keep going. We had no choice really, but I felt like giving up many times. It was really hard' (Interview 3). The following term, Lucy reflected on the cost to her wellbeing of constantly working and believing that she was irreplaceable. To protect her wellbeing and resilience, she aimed to take better care of herself so she could be there for her pupils.

> It's taking its toll on a lot of people. And I know people that have left the profession or were going to leave the profession just because of this last three months or so, and it's such a shame because obviously that's a lot of talented people that are going, but it has been very, very difficult. It's been really, really hard and there's been no break.
>
> *(Lucy, primary, Interview 4)*

Over two interviews, Cate described tearfully seeking support from her head teacher with what she felt was an unrealistic and unfair workload, but only receiving sympathy rather than any practical solutions. Cate was 'not enjoying work so much, the workload so much… bit fed up to be honest, a bit fed up' (Interview 3). She was also struggling to sleep 'because I've been working such long hours and I work into the evening, it's hard to switch off' (Interview 3). In her fourth interview, Cate was still struggling with her wellbeing as she had worked during the summer break to get her classroom ready for the new academic year and was still feeling very tired. Prior to the pandemic, she had thought about leaving her job because excessive workload was preventing her from having the life she wanted outside school, but now her wellbeing had declined to the point where 'this will be my last year in this school' (Interview 4) Cate described there being,

> more and more stressors all at once, it becomes all consuming. So, the littlest thing can sort of tip you over the edge. And I have had enough. I've told them that this will be my last year, I have said I would like to make it till July. The plan is to make it until July so that I can see this class out the door and go with them. If I feel like I can't manage though I won't hesitate to step out earlier for my mental health.
>
> *(Cate, primary, Interview 4)*

School leaders who foster supportive, trusting relationships with teachers can enhance their self-efficacy, commitment and resilience (Day et al., 2005). Yet, a minority of early-phase teachers in our study felt let down by their school leaders whom they saw as unsupportive, making poor decisions and creating unnecessary workload that negatively impacted on their wellbeing, resilience and commitment.

24 Building relationships, managing emotions

Decreased autonomy, increased scrutiny

Autonomy continues to be regarded by academics, teacher educators and teacher associations as a cornerstone of professionalism (Day et al., 2023), and is usually understood as the right of teachers to make individually determined judgments about teaching and learning in their classrooms. For Cate, who had decided to leave primary teaching and look for other work just before the pandemic hit, the first lockdown offered her greater autonomy and a reduced workload, leading to her to initially reconsider her decision and stay in her teaching post. However, Cate's renewed commitment to teaching quickly diminished as the school closures ended and senior leaders became concerned about pupil attainment and 'lost' learning. As her autonomy decreased, her workload and the scrutiny of her work intensified, prompting Cate to revert to her original plan to leave her teaching post and seek other work.

> When pupils returned to school after the first lockdown, Cate was given permission to be 'off timetable' and could focus on embedding basic skills, only moving on to something new when she felt pupils were ready.
>
>> We've had a lot more freedom. If anything, I've had more autonomy... because beforehand they were quite, 'you do this, at this time' and it was very structured, and I did feel like I had a lack of autonomy. I like being able to manage my lessons according to my class.
>>
>> *(Interview 2)*
>
> This shift meant Cate felt 'freer' (Interview 2) and, rather than leave her job at the end of the academic year, she asked her head teacher if she could stay in her current post.
>
> However, her feelings changed as the senior leadership team began to reduce her autonomy whilst increasing their scrutiny and control of her work. They implemented a video recording system in the classrooms and gave her a timetable of lessons each week that she had to film and send to subject leaders. She explained,
>
>> There's a lot of observation that happens, learning walks are constantly happening. You're constantly being scrutinised and there's always something. No matter how much you do, you could do better.
>>
>> *(Interview 4)*
>
> Cate's work was tightly controlled. 'We get told what we need to be teaching, given the learning objective' (Interview 3). She had to make sure that pupils produced a 'quality' piece of work for every subject every half term which meant cramming everything in. Cate felt that pupils would learn better and

Building relationships, managing emotions **25**

produce better work if she could focus on fewer subjects each term or was allowed to find ways to combine them, rather than following a curriculum devised by a subject leader. Her professional development was also tightly controlled. Cate lamented,

> There's not one week a staff meeting is cancelled. They'll always fill it with something and a lot of that is, look at this research and do that. So, it'd be nice to be given a choice about that though, as there are certain things I'm more interested in as a professional than others.
>
> *(Interview 4)*

Cate defined teacher professionalism as having autonomy to make decisions with the pupil's best interests at heart.

> Using my knowledge and my training as a teacher... trust has to be put into professionals that we actually want the best for children. And if you're using your knowledge and your training to actually put into practice what you believe is in the children's best interests, then you're a professional.
>
> *(Interview 4)*

> Being a professional is more about understanding what works in your classroom and using autonomy to make those decisions yourself... I think that people should have more trust in teachers to be professionals and have that autonomy instead of spending hours ticking boxes.
>
> *(Interview 4)*

Instead, senior leaders directed Cate to mark every piece of work, and to have a written plan for all her lessons. Cate thought a lot of what she was being asked to do was a waste of her time, and that she should be trusted to choose how best to use her time.

> If I don't think it's useful or valuable to extensively mark the books one day, then maybe we should be okay not having to ... if I don't want to write a full comment ... and I don't think it will help the children, maybe I should have the autonomy not to do that? Maybe I should have my own marking policy? Maybe I shouldn't have to fill in a planning sheet because... if the evidence is in the children's books that they're learning and I've supported them, if you can see that from looking at their books and talking to the children and watching my lessons, then why do I have to write it on a piece of paper?
>
> *(Interview 4)*

Cate recorded similar feelings in her journal, blaming unnecessary and greater control of her work for increasing her workload and preventing her from being the teacher she wanted to be (see Chapter 5).

Like Cate, Anna felt a lack of trust from school leaders who dictated her work. She would also have liked more autonomy to decide what her pupils needed, commenting,

> I care about my job. And I care about what needs to be done and I'll get what needs to be done, done. You know, the trust there was just shocking… really, really shocking. So, where's the autonomy?… It's missing. Trust. Trust is missing massively.
>
> *(Anna, secondary, Interview 4)*

Anna's experience of not feeling trusted by senior leaders and having initiatives forced on her without any discussion or gratitude, had made her reassess whether teaching would be a long-term career.

> It's definitely made me think, 'okay, so there might be a possibility where I look at this differently. And that I might want to go and do other things because I can understand why people are frustrated with it.' So, there's definitely been a bit of a question mark around this thing that I thought I was going to make my whole life, maybe it would be a portion of my life.
>
> *(Anna, secondary, Interview 4)*

As research has shown, trusting relationships between school leaders and teachers are important for teachers' motivation, commitment, resilience and effectiveness (Day et al, 2007; Day & Gu, 2010; Gu & Li, 2013). Teachers need to be able to make decisions about how to teach their pupils based on their training, experience, personality, and school context (Parker, 2015). The lack of autonomy and trust from school leaders that Cate and Anna experienced affected their motivation and commitment, prompting them to question whether they wanted to remain in the teaching profession.

Conclusion

Teachers' resilience

> is not primarily associated with the capacity to 'bounce back' or recover from highly traumatic experiences and events but, rather, the capacity to maintain equilibrium and a sense of commitment, agency and moral purpose in the everyday worlds in which teachers teach.
>
> *(Gu & Day, 2013, p. 26)*

For early-phase teachers, who were still learning to manage the everyday emotional and intellectual challenges that teachers experience, teaching during a pandemic should be understood as a traumatic experience. Multiple factors such as being isolated from pupils who were working from home, lacking contact and collaboration with colleagues, receiving negative feedback from parents, having few professional development opportunities and a reduced training year, dealing with challenging pupil behaviour, having to quickly develop new teaching approaches and resources and being unable to answer pupils' questions led to feelings of self-doubt and powerlessness which threatened their self-efficacy. They found teaching emotionally demanding, as they questioned whether they were letting pupils and parents down and worried about whether they were doing it 'right'.

In addition, some early-phase teachers expressed disappointment and frustration with senior leaders whom they viewed as unsupportive, lacking understanding, treating them as cogs in a machine, increasing workload and stress, having unrealistic expectations, not communicating effectively and not trusting them. Heavy workload had a significant impact on teachers' mental health and wellbeing, leaving them feeling exhausted and overwhelmed, not enjoying their job, and struggling to keep going. Combined with decreasing autonomy and a lack of trust from senior leaders, some teachers felt a reduced sense of professionalism and commitment to staying in the profession in the long-term.

However, the majority of early-phase teachers were buoyed by supportive relationships with the colleagues they worked closely with (see Chapter 8 for a more detailed discussion). Mutual support, reassurance, a sense of community and pulling together, sharing the load and a collegial culture rooted in trust, supported teachers' ability to keep going through this traumatic time. In addition, positive feedback from colleagues, pupils and parents led to feelings of achievement and pride which supported teachers' resilience and helped them to be optimistic that things would improve.

As Chapters 6 and 7 discuss further, the pandemic also shifted these teachers' understanding of teaching as primarily being about academic attainment, towards a deeper understanding of teaching as an emotional as well as academic endeavour. They quickly recognised the importance of caring for pupils' social and emotional wellbeing through building supportive relationships and being a role model. As the pandemic continued, it was this aspect of their role and the emotional bonds they had built with their pupils that became central, giving them a strong sense of purpose and motivation to teach to their best and to stay in the profession.

3

ADAPTING TO THE CHALLENGES

Mid-career teachers' perspectives

Introduction

The 18 mid-career primary and secondary school teachers whose voices are presented in this chapter had all taught for between seven and 23 years at the start of this study. Yet, despite their years of classroom experience, like all teachers they faced many new challenges caused by the pandemic. However, all had sustained or strengthened their sense of professional identity (see Chapter 6 for a detailed discussion) and commitment to their pupils; and, as with the early career phase teachers, they had found that care (Noddings, 2013) had become an increasingly important element of their work. The majority (13) spoke of the contribution of experiencing a positive school culture and strong professional relationships which had enabled them to sustain their wellbeing and job satisfaction over time. Nevertheless, like early career teachers, in the early stages of the pandemic they had struggled to manage the changes. As one mid-career secondary teacher remarked,

> When you've got this stress and the impact of a pandemic like Covid going on as well, and all the extra burdens that places on you, even teaching the hybrid lessons, you're dual planning, you're planning two lessons whenever a class has self-isolating students. It's made a lot of experienced staff feel like beginning teachers again.
>
> *(Neil, secondary, Interview 3)*

Managing uncertainties: adapting to new ways of working

The scale of the challenges that permeated these teachers' personal and professional lives was dramatic: fluctuating pupil engagement, social isolation,

DOI: 10.4324/9781003391661-3

home working, workload pressures, new technologies, increasingly vulnerable pupils, unpredictability of government decisions, the effects of incorporating safety restrictions into lessons: mask wearing, social distancing and limited equipment all served to de-stabilise long established routines and relationships and test teachers' capacities and capabilities.

Working from home was a huge adjustment for teachers who were accustomed to constant daily interaction with their pupils and colleagues. As many other professions found during homeworking, work life management became problematic as the clear divide between professional life at work and personal life at home became blurred. This impacted wellbeing initially, but most teachers were able to sustain their wellbeing over time and adapt.

The demands of a sudden reliance on technology created a challenge for all but one primary teacher, whereas all the secondary teachers felt confident and comfortable with using technology from the start of our research. However, Teresa showed no signs of being defeated.

> We're learning as we go along. My confidence levels are very low, but I'm learning. I'm doing [the] best I can.
>
> *(Teresa, primary, Interview 1)*

By the second interview Teresa marvelled at the new initiatives that the school developed, going forward.

> Some of the new ways of teaching and things like that [using technology], I was just amazed by it all.

Like all the teachers, they had become disheartened at times, but their resolve strengthened as they recognised the differences that they were able to make, particularly when pupils returned to school after lockdowns. They demonstrated an ability to adapt and persist. Thus, whilst emotional fluctuations and exhaustion were common, over the longer-term, they sustained their motivation, efficacy, and commitment.

> I think it's just new challenges and I've always wanted to teach, and I know that I make a difference and I think I do, at least. So, I guess it's just challenges that we've had to overcome… we just adapt and do it in a different way.
>
> *(Grace, primary, Interview 2)*

Some professional challenges differed depending on the school phase in which teachers worked. Technology, as we have seen, was only a challenge for primary teachers. This may reflect an expectation of more holistic online home learning packages offered to primary pupils from each teacher in primary schools.

30 Adapting to the challenges

Secondary teachers experienced different 'pinch points' regarding workload, particularly the intense workload pressures and uncertainties that teacher assessed grades (TAG) added to Year 11 (15–16 year olds) teachers' roles emerged in later terms. However, both primary and secondary teachers shared the experience of intensified workload during and following the second partial school closure.

> We have to constantly say to them 'we're still awaiting guidance' or 'this could change' or 'this is a draft' or 'this is what we might do', and it does feel as though you're kind of just stabbing in the dark sometimes.
>
> *(Gina, secondary, Interview 2)*

All secondary teachers struggled with fulfilling the role of reassuring their students during uncertainties, both during these uncertainties around cancelling GCSEs and in the first term when so much about the pandemic was still unknown. Primary teachers felt more confident in their role of creating normality for their children and providing the reassurance their younger learners needed.

Student engagement

Limited access to online teaching resources during the first lockdown, and inconsistent engagement with work at home were particularly prominent features of teachers responses: 'our children who always struggled anyway. So, for them, it was always going to be difficult' (Jane). In some cases previous progress seemed to be lost.

> It's like you're going up that slope, you get onto a plateau, and then you go up the next step. they've sort of stayed – it's the ones that are on that slope that have just gone right back to the bottom – with some of those, it is like you're starting from scratch again.
>
> *(Jane, primary, Interview 3)*

Teachers felt the weight of unrealistic expectations on their professional capacities, particularly following lockdowns or as groups of pupils were sent home to isolate. 'We lost the chance to teach face to face but some of the academic targets are still there' (Tim).

As pupils returned to full-time schooling, many struggled to get back into routines and behaviour for learning. Marion, a secondary teacher, found this to be her biggest challenge. She felt this had changed her role as a professional 'because students have kind of lost their thirst for knowledge' and she had to change her teaching as a result.

Simultaneously, safety restrictions such as mask wearing, social distancing and limiting equipment restricted teachers' ability to engage their learners.

It was like teaching a class of zombies... you just had all these like really dark eyes looking at you from above a mask and no responses in class and no interaction... it just was a very unhappy place to be teaching and it was almost like trying to be an entertainer at a wake sometimes and that was tough.

(Neil, secondary, Interview 4)

Managing external threats

Mistrust in the government also challenged many teachers, threatening their motivation and professional confidence. Barbara felt that this had threatened her role as a professional.

I think there's a tremendous amount of frustration, not just me but all teachers, with just the way the government have handled everything – it's been absolutely the most ridiculous thing I've ever seen.

(Barbara, secondary, Interview 1)

Neil, however, dismissed the government discourse of 'catching up' with 'lost learning' and remained confident in his own abilities to make a difference.

Catching up to where we expected they would have been seems, for me, foolish, because that implies that what we were doing before was that inefficient, that we can somehow squeeze that much more back out of them.

(Neil, secondary, Interview 2)

Margaret described risk assessments and strategic decision making around government guidelines.

As new guidance came out and new figures were out, we were constantly having to reach, check stuff and shimmy things around.

(Margaret, primary, Interview 1)

Gina, like most mid-career teachers, was able to successfully negotiate the challenges.

GINA, GREENFIELDS SECONDARY

The most surreal, intense and stressful time for Gina had been the two weeks before the first national lockdown. With the head teacher ill, staff looked to her and her senior leadership team [SLT] at this unsettling time. Gina had found the pace of change too much to absorb at first. She developed new routines and practices at short notice. She was frustrated at last minute government announcements and muddled through. Yet, despite the pressures, Gina was

32 Adapting to the challenges

motivated, feeling 'galvanised', by the positive impact of her role on 'thriving' staff, supporting them through uncertain times.

The most 'joyous moment' came as pupils returned to school after negative tests. She was concerned by the achievement gap widening for the most vulnerable pupils, who were often the ones not engaging with home learning. Her relationships with parents strengthened through their role in pupils' home learning and Gina's confidence improved further as parents expressed their gratitude for the schools' efforts.

While Gina recognised the first lockdown as a period of creativity for teachers, tensions later arose following the second partial school closure as more rigid structures returned. Her optimism, however, once again waned as teachers felt unsupported when lesson observations resumed, and Gina belatedly recognised that managerial decisions had not been communicated effectively.

Relationships with pupils: commitment and care

Teachers' roles differed considerably in terms of their responsibilities and contact with parents and guardians of children during lockdown. For Alan, a primary school teacher, relationships with his pupils and the wider school community were fundamental to his motivation.

> I was in charge of finding the vulnerable children's families and talking to them, and that's a great honour. It is a privilege doing that.
>
> *(Alan, primary, Interview 1)*

As with early career teachers, Teresa's care for pupils had become the most important driver for her ongoing commitment.

> I've always been really committed to my job, and I would still say that I am really committed to my job.... I do have days where I come home and think I'm leaving. But then the next day I go back in and see the children again... I know that we make a big difference.
>
> *(Teresa, primary, Interview 3)*

Although Emma, Theo, and Barbara did not sustain their commitment to their current schools, together with all teachers in the project, they shared a sustained commitment to their pupils.

> [I am] still really strongly committed to the kids, I feel that I make a difference every day to the children, that's what drives me.
>
> *(Emma, primary, Interview 4)*

Barbara was also determined to do a good job for her pupils.

I have always been 100% committed, and can you go higher than 100%? I feel much more committed... because in 5, 10 years it will be like 'oh they were the Covid kids'... and I want to make sure that they have everything that they need.

(Barbara, secondary, Interview 4)

The importance of workplace relationships

Teachers across all phases valued relationships characterised by trust with leaders and colleagues, which contributed to sustaining commitment and wellbeing (see also Chapter 8). A sense of collegiality became increasingly important during the pandemic, as lockdowns and restrictions created social isolation in teachers' personal lives. This had a profound impact on subjective wellbeing for these mid-career teachers as personal relationships with friends and family were constrained by restrictions on personal lives. Social capital, the psychological and practical gains originating from the goodwill within relationships (Adler & Kwon, 2002), was a crucial resource for teachers as they navigated professional challenges by working together and supporting each other (see also Chapter 8 for a more detailed discussion).

Supportive work environments were especially important for those who were socially isolated in their personal lives.

> Providing that space to talk [is important] because some of our teachers, they live at home on their own. Sometimes you know coming into school we're the only people that they see because they're not allowed to go and see anybody else.
>
> *(Teresa, primary, Interview 2)*

Restrictions to interactions at work made things more difficult. Georgina, a secondary teacher struggled with the strategic differences in operating in these new ways.

> I like to do things in a certain way and get everyone on board and team build-ing and get people together and at the moment we've not been able to do that.
> *(Georgina, secondary, Interview 1)*

Positive relationships with colleagues were an important source for well-being, a sense of community and belonging that helped teachers feel valued and supported.

> It's been a very supportive place... If any of us is struggling, we will talk to each other. And I think we're lucky because we've got that really strong team around us.
>
> *(Teresa, primary, Interview 3)*

34 Adapting to the challenges

This collegiality influenced teachers' capacity for sustaining their resilience. Alan had struggled to sustain his wellbeing due to health anxiety, but his colleagues enabled him to persevere.

> I think for me, working with the person I've been working with in school has helped me to overcome a lot of the issues that I've had working during this time. It's been good to be able to share, share that load, and also to persevere I suppose, and to come to work against the fear that you have.
>
> *(Alan, primary, Interview 2)*

Contact with others, in both personal and professional spheres, was deeply missed by many teachers.

> I always thought that one of the really positive things about teaching was having staff meetings together and going to the staff room and spending time with other staff members, and a lot of that has gone because you can't really socialize with many other year groups.
>
> *(Tim, primary, Interview 2)*

Neil admitted that the job was less enjoyable without this interaction.

> That's really hard just because you thrive off those interactions – passing in the corridor, sitting down in the staff room, having a coffee with someone you've not seen for a week or so.
>
> *(Neil, secondary, Interview 2)*

Despite the challenges posed by restrictions on physical interactions, relationships with colleagues and leaders remained important. Where these were perceived as present within school leadership, and collegiality was stronger, teachers felt valued and experienced a sense of belonging.

> The quality and clarity of communication has been quite amazing. There's a common feeling that there has been a real transparency about how the situation has been handled. It's not been a 'top-down' situation. It has been very much, 'This is the decision process. We are trying our best to manage the situation, because no one knows what's going to happen. We've never dealt with this before, but this is what we are doing... everyone felt that we were in this together.
>
> *(Neil, secondary, Interview 1)*

Gina, an teacher with leadership responsibilities at the same school, agreed.

If something's got on top of everybody or there's a real issue, they will say to us and we will listen and do something about it, because that's where you need to step in and change things.

(Gina, secondary, Interview 2)

The impact of positive communication from school senior leadership teams on teachers' motivation and moral purpose had enabled them to feel valued within the challenging circumstances in which they worked.

You assuage some of the fear-mongering, because everyone had the opportunity to contribute. That was a very nice approach to navigate some of the issues that we were facing. What was very clear was that although the interests of the pupils were at the heart of everything we did, there was definitely an awareness of maintaining teachers' wellbeing throughout.

(Neil, secondary, Interview 1)

Fostering these relationships was crucial for maintaining a positive school culture, sustaining teachers' wellbeing and their motivation to stay in post. Where this was not the case, commitment declined. Theo felt unsupported in his school due to a wide gap between senior leaders and middle leaders. He had gone on to secure a job at a different school.

Efficacy and agency

People have always striven to exercise control over events that affect their lives. They seek control because it provides them with countless personal and social benefits. Uncertainty in things that have significant personal consequences is highly unsettling…Inability to exert influence over things that adversely affect one's life breeds apprehension, dysfunction, apathy and despair.

(Bandura, 2000, p. 16)

Efficacy and agency were key characteristic of most of these mid-career teachers, working together as protective layers; agency and efficacy serve to promote hope of success; and resilience energises inner motivational frameworks (Keogh et al, 2012).

Teacher efficacy, defined as 'teachers' beliefs about their capability to impact students' motivation and achievement' (Tschannen-Moran & Hoy, 2001, p. 2), has long been associated with traits of successful teaching, pupil achievement and teacher resilience (Goddard et al, 2004; Kim & Seo, 2018). Tschannen-Moran and Hoy claim that efficacy

36 Adapting to the challenges

> affects the effort they invest in teaching, the goals they set, and their level of aspiration... teachers' persistence when things do not go smoothly and their resilience in the face of setbacks.
>
> *(Tschannen-Moran & Hoy, 2001, p. 783)*

For many teachers, a sense of collective efficacy was engrained within their workplace relationships, and had a particularly important role within teacher wellbeing, for example with teachers working collectively within their departments to make decisions.

> People do not live their lives in isolation. Many of the things they seek are achievable only through socially interdependent effort. Hence, they have to work in coordination with others to secure what they cannot accomplish on their own.
>
> *(Bandura, 2001, p. 13)*

As middle-phase teachers, their many years of professional experience provided a resource to help navigate challenges with a degree of confidence. They were able to draw upon their years of experience, their understanding of children's learning needs and accumulated attitudes and strategies, to manage the strains of high workloads on personal lives.

Applying this experience relied on *agency*: feeling enabled to intentionally, 'play a part in their self-development, adaptation, and self-renewal with changing times' (Bandura, 2001, p. 2). Agency comes in different forms, 'direct personal agency, proxy agency that relies on others to act on one's behest to secure desired outcomes, and collective agency exercised through socially coordinative and interdependent effort' (Bandura, 2001, p. 1).

The communal nature of collective agency had a particularly significant impact on wellbeing overtime. Collective efficacy strengthened and galvanised teaching teams. As existing research has established, when a groups' collective efficacy is higher, 'the higher the groups' aspirations and motivational investment in their undertakings, the stronger their staying power in the face of impediments and setbacks, the higher their morale and resilience to stressors, and the greater their performance accomplishments' (Bandura, 2001, p. 14).

> Most of them [the pupils] wanted to come to school or appreciated it when they came back. So, I think as a professional, I feel certainly more valued by young people, and appreciated by young people.
>
> *(Gina, secondary, Interview 4)*

With professional experience to draw on, most teachers were willing and able to adapt, in order to make a difference for their pupils.

I've been doing this job a long time now, and it changes – you just have to adapt with the change and go with what they say, and you just turn up and do the best that you can for the kids every day.

(Jane, primary, Interview 3)

At Greenfields Secondary, Mark and Neil exercised direct personal agency (Bandura, 2001) to manage their workloads effectively.

[I put in] a solid shift and get a certain level of results and you can then almost double that, almost kill yourself and get a little bit more. And it's realising that that little bit more is not worth sacrificing your own life for, because if you did... I wouldn't be in the profession now and I like to think that I add value to the profession still.

(Neil, secondary, Interview 3)

And it's probably taken me 30 odd years to get to that point, but I no longer allow the school, or the pressures attached to it, to dictate anything I do once I leave the school building.

(Mark, secondary, Interview 3)

Professional isolation: the limitations of going it alone

Although over time most middle phase teachers' wellbeing was robust, anchored within teacher identity (see Chapter 6) and the collective moral endeavour to make a positive difference to their pupils, for a minority, (4) wellbeing was low and could not be recovered.

These teachers were isolated from the sense of belonging within the school community in some way as their relationships with leaders and/or colleagues eroded (see Chapter 8). Mark, secondary, and Emma, primary, were both clinically vulnerable, and were shielding at home as their colleagues returned to school during periods of whole school reopening.

At the moment, I kind of feel very disconnected from school, from my colleagues. I feel a bit forgotten.

(Emma, primary, Interview 2)

Emma described professional loneliness, as she became distanced from her colleagues, particularly her best friend at work. This had a profound impact on her sense of belonging 'I don't belong. I don't belong anywhere at the minute'. Mark also felt, 'completely abandoned, out of the loop... I haven't really got a clue what's really going on in school.'

The breakdown of Theo and Barbara's relationship with school leaders at Valley View had a negative impact on their wellbeing and commitment (see Chapter 8). Trust had diminished and they did not feel invested in many of

38 Adapting to the challenges

their school's policies and practices. They struggled to navigate the pupil wellbeing policy alongside the pressure of academic progress.

> At the moment we're in a situation where it's just like blanket sympathy – here's a time-out pass... it's actually well, we are still a school, responsible for their learning.
>
> *(Theo, secondary, Interview 3)*

Theo felt restrained by the approach of his leaders. He had lost confidence in them.

> You can't say anything because you feel like you're not being sufficiently empathetic.... Surely, we should be doing more than just a card. It seems like just a plaster over a huge crack.
>
> *(Theo, secondary, Interview 3)*

Despite recognising the positive impact of their work on pupils at times, Theo and Barbara were less able to resolve challenges than other middle-phase teachers, who experienced a stronger sense of belonging and had more trust in their leaders (13).

Barbara also felt frustrated by government decisions. Last minute changes imposed by the exam regulator, Ofqual left her 'scrambling' to get work back from pupils. She was disconnected from school management, who she thought were unsupportive and 'live in a bubble'. She described 'lost learning' as 'a shambles' Her school's educational philosophy and priorities also felt at odds with her own.

A capacity for resilience

Whilst individual and collective efficacy and agency were fundamental elements which contributed to these mid-career teachers' ability to survive and flourish, it was their capacities for resilience which made this possible over time. Research has revealed how interwoven teachers' worlds and work are, and how teacher resilience has both individual and collective elements to it. Early professional life phases teachers considered pupil behaviour more of a challenge, whilst mid-career teachers were less affected. Lack of parental support and government policies undoubtedly frustrated these teachers, causing fluctuations in their capacities for resilience. However, these failed to have a long-term impact on these teachers. Where professional relationships were strong teachers were able to negotiate the challenges.

In addition, as we have illustrated in this chapter, there were significant differences in these middle career teachers' personal life circumstances which shaped their experiences during the pandemic. Many teachers with young children at home had additional pressures, and those living alone tended to be

Adapting to the challenges **39**

more isolated and lonelier during lockdowns. A minority of teachers with health conditions experienced heightened safety fears and additional restraints within their lives which intensified the challenges of the pandemic. When Dan, a secondary school teacher, returned to school following the first lockdown, his wife was simultaneously receiving treatment for a serious health condition. That, together with family duties and workload pressures, resulted in his being able only to have five hours sleep a night. It is not surprising that, despite dedication to his pupils and profession, Dan experienced heightened pressures on maintaining his wellbeing.

> I love being a teacher, because this gives me an opportunity to bring so much to my children and inspire them. And myself, I think this is the only thing I can do – I'm a born teacher…This is really tough, because I have no choice but to do work, but then I have no choice to look after my family, so it's been really, really stressful.
>
> *(Dan, secondary, Interview 1)*

These personal circumstances influenced and interacted with teachers' professional worlds. Those with physical health conditions, Emma, and Mark, were unable to sustain their wellbeing overtime as they experienced the pandemics' challenges acutely. Other differences were usually mediated by teachers as they utilised their workplace relationships and dedication to their profession to navigate through their circumstances. School leaders who took account of teachers' individual situations were highly valued (see Chapter 8 for a more detailed discussion).

> Capacities to be resilient were influenced not only by their biographies and the strength of their educational values, but also by factors embedded in the socio-cultural and policy contexts of teaching and in different personal, relational and organisational conditions of their work and lives.
>
> *(Gu & Day, 2013, p. 23)*

Most teachers (13) were able to draw upon reserves of energy to sustain their wellbeing over time (see also Chapter 5). Although the challenges of adapting to changes over which they had no control caused fluctuations in their levels of self-efficacy and agency, positive school cultures, characterised by strong professional relationships, and an inner motivation to help increasingly vulnerable pupils, enabled all these teachers to remain committed to their professional roles, adapting to the pandemic's seemingly endless challenges with the tenacity and drive they credited to a strong individual and collective moral purpose.

Conclusion

As this chapter has shown, these middle phase teachers faced a barrage of challenges throughout the two-year period, but adapted to fulfil their professional obligations.

40 Adapting to the challenges

They continued to engage with and support increasingly vulnerable pupils, and managed government announcements, public expectations, and changes in workplace conditions with success. The overwhelming majority of teachers experienced an incredible capacity for resilience through this, demonstrating unwavering commitment to their pupils, roles and schools. They drew strength from their relationships with colleagues and leaders, and their professional conviction to care and support their learners. With between seven and 23 years of experience to draw upon, they had more confidence in their professional capacities than some early phase teachers. Their self-efficacy was less fragile, as was their sense of confidence in their ability to make a difference, and their capacities for to draw on their capacities for resilience. All were key elements of their professionalism.

4

TEACHING AS SERVICE

Later-career teachers' perspectives

Introduction

This chapter explores how six later phase teachers, four primary and two secondary, with over 23 years of teaching experience, responded to the pandemic. The chapter begins by reporting these teachers' renewal of commitment to their long-held ethics of teaching as service, expressed through the positive ways in which they responded to changes in their working conditions. In contrast to those in early and mid-career phases, from the beginning they spoke of their willingness to embrace change, driven by a strong sense of moral purposes, their sense of oneness with their pupils and families and their loyalty to the schools in which they worked, as key drivers of their professionalism.

Moral purpose: commitment to core values

Rose and Sandra, secondary teachers, both stated that they were intending to leave the profession at the beginning of the pandemic. However, as the pandemic 'season' progressed both had become more committed to their teaching, overcoming personal and external challenges. Teaching pre-supposes that teachers actively engage in pupil's learning (Pring, 2021). For these teachers, however, it was more than simply enacting a set of pre-defined actions that they used to foster pupil's learning. They were teachers for whom teaching was an integral part of their life, and for whom teaching had always been, and remained a passion (Liston & Garrison, 2004). They showed a passion for their pupils, their pupil's learning, their schools, their communities and the teaching profession itself. They confirmed evidence from other research on the moral purposes of teaching by devoting themselves to finding ways to help their pupils directly

DOI: 10.4324/9781003391661-4

42 Teaching as service

through their reports of their daily classroom practice through the formal curriculum, and indirectly throughout the school-life course (Campbell, 2008a; Mart, 2013). In other words, their daily actions of fairness, kindness, honesty and respect to their pupils and communities were a reflection of their moral purposes (Campbell, 2003).

Fern, a primary teacher, had a strong commitment since the beginning of the pandemic. For her, commitment referred not just to teaching but to a sense of moral purpose to serve pupils and their communities

> I love my job, it's as simple as that. No two days are the same. A lot of what I deal with on a day-to-day basis has absolutely nothing to do with teaching – being in a school is not just about teaching, it's being part of a community, a family – and that is what keeps me going even when things are tough. And things have been tough this past year.
>
> *(Fern, primary, later, Journal 1)*

Her commitment had become even stronger throughout the pandemic when she reported that she was even more keen to know what children need – 'You can actually see what it is that you need the children to learn'. She attributed her change in thinking due to the pandemic 'I've got a slightly different mindset about a few things now' (Interview 4).

Fern and other later phase teachers seemed to have responded to the crisis by re-committing themselves to pupils and teaching. Like Fern, many attributed this to the strong moral purpose that they had developed over time long before the pandemic.

For example, Dawn, another primary teacher, described her commitment as, 'scoring "10 out of 10", because I've been so committed to trying to get these children up to where they should be' (Interview 3).

Likewise, Michelle, also primary school teacher, associated her responses with her core moral purposes

> Despite the many challenges of teaching, I enjoy seeing children grow socially, emotionally and academically. Seeing the positive impact I can have on children and their families inspires me every day....They need us more than ever. And there's a greater reason to be the best teacher that you can be more than ever....Being able to do your job the best that you can, in spite of any circumstances that might be around you, whether they're the circumstances in your immediate environment or circumstances in the wider world. So yeah, I think the word that comes to me in my head is 'consistency' that no matter what's going on, you have to deal with what those children get.
>
> *(Michelle, primary, later, Interview 3)*

Sara, a primary teacher, also spoke of becoming even more committed since the pandemic began, despite being in the 'twilight of her career'

I really enjoyed my career, always. It's something I always wanted to do, and now I'm hoping as I get towards the twilight of my career that I'm hoping to head back more into the classroom and do more teaching and less management stuff over the next few years.

(Sara, primary, later, Interview 1)

She felt even more determined to ensure that the children were happy and positive, and that their learning losses were minimised. Although working long hours (from 7am to 9pm most days) and all weekends, she was still there to help her pupils

I love my job, so I'd say 10 [out of 10 for motivation]. I still love the job, Love the kids... this is my 36th year so it's not going to put me off.

(Sara, primary, later, Interview 3)

Confidence: **as long held and practised ethics of teaching as service**

For me, COVID-19 is just another chapter in my teaching career.

(Dawn, primary, later, Journal 1)

These teachers' belief in teaching as service was expressed through what they said about their confidence in being able to draw upon their ability to manage change successfully.

Sara and Rose had found transition to online learning challenging at the beginning. However, later they both asserted that 'when you've been teaching as long as I have you take it completely in your stride' (Rose, secondary, later, Interview 1). While Sara commented that 'it is just getting on and doing it really' (Sara, primary, later, Interview 4).

Sandra felt that her teaching practices were 'not as different as I thought' (Interview 1), and that the challenges had influenced her to be more reflective in terms of her teaching. Having to adapt her teaching had made her also reflect on how to teach certain topics as a department.

If children had missed a certain poem, do we need to teach them that again or do we move on and have to bear in mind that they've missed out some practice and development?

(Sandra, secondary, later, Interview 2)

As with others in this career phase, her confidence had increased even more over the course of the pandemic.

You know why you're doing the job; you know what you want from the students, you know what your purpose is, but you also know that they're not

44 Teaching as service

necessarily going to be on the same page as you, and you've got to carry on as if they have.

(Sandra, secondary, later, Interview 4)

Michelle's positive attitudes around the changes happening in her work had increased throughout the pandemic

If anything, some of the good things that came out of [the] previous lockdown have continued.... It wasn't too hard then to kind of flip everything to being remote learning.

(Michelle, primary, later, Interview 1)

As the period of the pandemic extended, Michelle's confidence appeared to grow even stronger 'I would say my classroom practice hasn't been affected. Certainly, hasn't been affected in a negative way' (Interview 2); and she claimed to feel 'even more creative than I think we are' (Interview 2).

That immediate jump to online learning … that was a massive change, and it wasn't a negative impact by any means.... Like a lot of things, it's turned from a negative into a positive.

(Michelle, primary, later, Interview 4)

Fern was confident throughout the pandemic

As a leader of a school, we had to give out the impression that we were in control and that we knew what was happening … we had to keep up as best as we could.

(Fern, primary, later, Journal 1)

She maintained her confidence to make a difference to pupil's lives, attributing it to her experience

Some days I've gone 'Right okay, tell me what the latest new challenge is, and we'll sort it, and we'll move on'. I'm not sure everybody would have been able to have just stepped up and organize things in the way that I have done, and I think that's because I have the experience to draw on.

(Fern, primary, later, Interview 4)

The evidence from all in the project, but especially pronounced in these later career teachers, suggests that teaching was viewed as more than just a job. That they are unable to distinguish between their moral selves and their professional selves. These positions served as a moral framework for their reasoning which informed their interactions with pupils, giving them hope for the future (Tirri, 2010). They perceived teaching as an ethically driven service and had developed a professional responsibility to serve their pupils, their pupil's parents, and their communities (Campbell, 2008b).

Care for pupils and families

The pandemic made huge demands upon teachers' emotional resilience, challenging existing relationships 'love, care and solidarity, that enable people to lead successful lives' (Lynch & Walsh, 2009).Yet, these later phase teachers seemed to relish the opportunities provided to focus on caring for both for the emotional and the academic needs of their pupils. Caring in this sense refers to the development and positive responses to the whole development of a child (see Chapter 7 for a more detailed discussion of care). Before the start of the pandemic, Sandra was intending to retire due to her age. As the pandemic progressed, however, her commitment to her pupils made her rethink that she could not retire, at least until the following year, because her pupils really needed her.

> I'm sort of thinking well I can't really retire next year, because this current year group, they really need to have somebody who knows what they're doing. So, I can't go until I've got everyone sorted out.
>
> *(Sandra, secondary, later, Interview 2)*

Rose was also intending to retire at the start of the pandemic. However, as the pandemic progressed, she had become more focused on helping her pupils 'catch up' with their lost learning, and 'didn't have the headspace' to think about retirement. Her re-commitment became more explicit as the pandemic progressed, when she stated that her biggest regret over the last two years was the missed learning opportunities for her pupils. Rose had also revisited her values, realising that it was more important to her for pupils to acquire the basic skills they would need for a successful life ahead

> Does it really matter that some of the kids have missed out on scheme of work on Black Death or Easter? It's not going to change their lives. It's about making sure they're not getting wound up and upset about not doing that. It's about ensuring that they understand the basic skills, irrelevant of what the topic is – making sure the skills are there.
>
> *(Rose, secondary, later, Interview 2)*

Michelle spoke about the equal opportunities given to children through online teaching, creating a space where every child felt more comfortable to express themselves.

> It was wonderful, seeing a new side to some children because their voice was finally equal to some other classmates, and they felt in a safe space

46 Teaching as service

and place to be themselves. Without doubt, we were engaging in more one to one dialogue with some children who were more comfortable using their voice through the medium of IT. It was wonderful, seeing some children's new passions, interests and actively encouraging them to pursue and share them with us as a way of keeping them engaged with online and connected to the school community.

(Michelle, primary, later, Journal 1)

Michelle also believed that providing emotional support for pupils would help accelerate their academic progress 'Socially and behaviourally first, because if the child is where they should be socially, if you like, academically they can advance more easily.' (Interview 2). Throughout the two-years of the research period, she emphasised the importance of caring for children who struggled more once they were back in school.

And the first thing that we do is mentally you 'clock' that child on a daily basis when they enter the room, … knowing that particular pupil's journey, … And then it's just about getting the balance right every day with them. And actually, it's about including them, because they've probably been largely ignored at home because their parents have had better things on.

(Michelle, primary, later, Interview 3)

Sara spoke of how important it was for her to organise something for her pupils that she knows would make them feel excited.

Last week we returned from a trip nearby, where we all went in full Victorian clothes, and we had a full day of games and going around the court. And then on Friday we had a full Victorian classroom day. So, you could do the basic stuff every day, which is fine. But every now and again to do something that's exciting or different. It's those things that the children remember at the end of the day.

(Sara, primary, later, Interview 4)

For Fern, it was the youngest pupils who needed the most support

The biggest issue now is the children coming in in early years… they've not played with their cousins. They've not been and sat in their mum's front room whilst their mates come around with their little one. Then sometimes they weren't able to go and play on the park, they haven't been able to go to playgroups… So…. [we need] to try and backfill and target those early years children. Otherwise, it's in the next 10 years that they're going to come through school and they're going to have missed vital stuff.

(Fern, primary, later, Interview 4)

Support for the more vulnerable

Later phase teachers also spoke of their care not only for pupils but also their families. They took initiatives to monitor vulnerable families and provided children with academic and emotional support throughout the pandemic. Fern spoke emotionally about how COVID-19 had affected 'vulnerable' families who could not access support from social services. She had been 'given permission that actually caring for the children and their families.... is important because otherwise you can't move them forward academically. It's strengthened my philosophy' (Interview 1). The same case of caring for pupils applied to her colleagues in her school who were all making welfare calls to vulnerable pupils.

Dawn spoke about how her school responded effectively to support vulnerable pupils. 'We were able to provide a high-class quality education to children as normal. The care and communication with vulnerable children continued in the same exemplary way as always.' (Journal 2). Additionally, she referred to the importance of parental engagement in supporting pupils academically. For Dawn, the children who had not engaged with the online provision did not have encouraging parents, and were working at lower attainment levels.

> Seeing children who were doing well falling behind with their learning. The fact that some children did little or no work during lockdown was a concern to me professionally.
>
> *(Dawn, primary, later, Journal 2)*

She and her colleagues made weekly phone calls to the families of all the children to see what help they might need.

> I know my worth and that individuals at school and at Trust level have gone out of their way to ensure that our pupils and their families have had as much support as they have needed to keep going.
>
> *(Dawn, primary, later, Journal 3)*

Sara, like Dawn, phoned parents each week offering help, and if this didn't have an effect, she had invited children into school. Those who remained at home but did not engage, were targeted with more interventions to help them 'catch up'

> We were phoning up any children that didn't engage every week and saying Can we help?' 'What's what? What is the issue? Is there a problem?' Then, if it continued, we often invited those children to come to school... We got a lot of those pupils into school if they weren't accessing from home...
>
> *(Sara, primary, later, Interview 2)*

48 Teaching as service

Doing the best that you can do to set a good example for the kids and to give the kids the best possible opportunities that they can have to make the best of themselves in the future.

(Sara, primary, later, Interview 4)

When Rose, a secondary teacher, realised that there were issues with the English government's food voucher scheme that was intended to support vulnerable households by providing them with vouchers at the same time as parents were losing their jobs, she had set up a foodbank showing her strong care for pupils and their families.

> I sat in a meeting in late April 2020 and heard that one of our families had contacted school because they were in severe financial difficulties because they had no money for food and were having problems accessing the voucher scheme. At this point, every time I did a supermarket shop, I was making a substantial contribution to their food bank. I contacted the head and said I would be happy to provide a parcel for one or two of our families (if this was appropriate) or to go a stage further and set up a food bank in school. We went down the food bank option and successfully supported up to 25 families from May 2020 until the end of the summer term. I was also able to organise help for the families through a summer food scheme, with several of our staff being involved. Whilst this started from a very negative experience, it became a huge positive with staff, students and the local community, some with no connection to the school, became involved in supporting the scheme. We also made a decision to provide food parcels and little gifts for our families for Christmas 2020, where with help again from staff, students and the community, we delivered parcels to 35 families on the last two days of term before Christmas. The original aim of doing the food bank was to help families in need (and for the same reason another member of staff made numerous visors for NHS staff and carers during the first lockdown). We have subsequently been recognised for what we have achieved and were awarded from our community for that.
>
> *(Rose, primary, later, Journal 3)*

Her commitment became more obvious from the fact that she was trying to provide as much support needed to every pupil to arrange their work placements. She described how anxious she was that only 25% of her pupils were offered work placements, compared to a much higher proportion two years previously. At that time, she didn't know whether she would let those with placements go or postpone them till later in year so more of the year group could take part.

Loyalty to school

The degree to which teachers felt integrated with colleagues and students at their schools has been closely associated with their sense of belonging (Skaalvik & Skaalvik, 2011). This was closely associated with their strong loyalty (Slaten et al., 2016). Their schools were their reference points both when they needed support and when they wanted to provide support to their colleagues. Throughout the pandemic this was evidenced through colleague support, strong bonding with colleagues, effective school organisation and a strong sense of being part of a team. Michelle commented for her senior leadership team at her school that 'There is a good balance between conversation and direction' (Interview 1). The importance of Michelle's professional relationships with colleagues was made even clearer when she characterised her colleagues as her 'team' (Interview 2). Joint discussions with senior management in the school had enabled her to overcome heavy workload issues, navigate her work life management and maintain her professional health throughout pandemic

> I work with a great team of teachers and it's why I'm at the school without a doubt, because there's a lot of teaching jobs out there. The school is quite a distance from my house. It's not a particularly easy drive, but I 100% trust the colleagues that I work with. We learn from each other, and we learn through each other, and we laugh together. We cry together. We know when each other needs support.... I think the whole thing made me feel even more a greater sense of one's position within a community. Whether that's your colleagues, the people that turn up every day, or whether that's the families of the children that you serve every day.
>
> *(Michelle, primary, later, Interview 4)*

Fern, also showed a great loyalty to her school. At the start of the project, she confessed missing having 'a cup of coffee and a chat' with her colleagues and singing with them in school assemblies. In the same way, she supported a newly qualified teacher who had missed out on important teaching experiences since most of her teaching career was within the pandemic.

As the pandemic progressed, Fern took the initiative of covering the absence of support services for children in her school for a long time, and offered in-school support where she could, for example 'rejigging' staffing. She had also put some assembly songs on a recording, and had held an outside assembly – 'The children were crying as they realised – a few of them were just like "Oh, we're just all together singing our songs again"' (Interview 3). Fern reflected that bringing the school together as a community was important. Before the pandemic she had found assemblies an annoying part of her job, but she had really missed them – 'it's the getting together of the children... all of the children in the same place.' (Interview 3)

50 Teaching as service

Sara was proud of how her school had responded to the many challenges.

> I'm quite proud of what we did …we try to take things and then we adapt them so that it best fits our school …because we are a community school, and we want to make sure that all our parents and children get the best deal that they can. So basically, we've done what we've been asked to do. We've really stuck to the letter of the law, and but we've made it our own in the way that we've implemented it…we follow the rules, but we've also made it personal to make sure it fits our kids and our parents, and our community.
>
> *(Sara, primary, later, Interview 1)*

She confessed that she was 'putting a brave face on' for her colleagues –'even if you're not feeling wonderful. You've got to try and make sure that you are smiley and happy and positive… And make sure that you look after anybody else as well, so it's part of being that team person really.' (Interview 1) Sara was feeling that her head teacher had looked after staff –'It's been so stressful for the head teacher. I think she she's diverted a lot of it away from us, so I think she's taking a lot of that onto her own shoulders.' (Interview 1). She revealed that in her school they had set up a wellbeing committee with responsibility for organising wellbeing activities to support her colleagues' mental health

> We have recently we set up a wellbeing committee that has six members of staff on it and actually, we meet quite regularly. So, every couple of weeks we arranged activities for the staff to do 'cause we felt that we were a bit isolated from each other. So we did outdoor bed and outdoor hot chocolate and marshmallows over the fire 'cause we have a great forest school.
>
> *(Sara, primary, later, Interview 3)*

On a more positive note, it [COVID-19] highlighted the importance of great colleagues.

(Dawn, primary, later, Journal 1)

Dawn, was proud of how her school responded to pupil's needs caring for their future education

> Goldfinch Primary has built a recovery curriculum in a well-developed way, so that pupils are taught accurately but without overloading them (or their teachers) with work. It understands the needs of pupils and the wider educational community so that future education is not impeded by anything implemented at this point.
>
> *(Dawn, primary, later, Journal 3)*

She spoke of how her school was incorporating digital learning in responding to the needs of future education

> Learning from past experiences, society will need to work harder to help children adapt to the new norms in a post-lockdown world. This means the future of education will be increasingly focused on digital literacy. We, at Goldfinch Primary, will need to determine a digital methodology and effectively communicate it to all those involved.
>
> *(Dawn, primary, later, Journal 3)*

Her loyalty to her school was not only limited to pupils, but also to her school colleagues and those in the other schools. They collaborated within a networked system, and with other stakeholders to ensure the value of the child in the community, as well as that the collective actions of all civic actors protect high-quality education.

Dawn was appreciative of the way her school and her Trust had handled things 'I just think everything has really been very positive and done really well.' (Interview 1). She reflected that her bonding with her colleagues had become even stronger since the pandemic and highlighted the support from the senior leadership team in her school and the support from the Trust for all her colleagues in her school.

> The school and the Trust have supported us with providing online drop-in sessions for people feeling the strain, suggestions for activities and hobbies to take up if feeling under par and the knowledge that there is always someone at the end of a phone if we need anything. SLT [Senior Leadership Team] have been particularly good at letting staff know they are available anytime.
>
> *(Dawn, primary, later, Journal 3)*

The SLT support was also expressed through mental health support to colleagues.

> There are always people that you can talk to. There's always a support system here, and even when we're working at home senior leadership says, 'Is there anything we can do? Do you want anything? We just want to chat if you're on your own.'
>
> *(Dawn, primary, later, Interview 3)*

Conclusion

Later phase teachers responded to the turbulences in their working conditions and threats to their professional identities caused by the pandemic with a strong confidence in their abilities to overcome all the challenges that were

52 Teaching as service

presented. Their strong determination and confidence derived in part from experience, a strong sense of 'belonging', both to their schools and the communities which they served, and a clear belief in teaching as service, and was expressed through the active, sustained cognitive, social, and emotional support. This strong moral compass in caring for pupils and their families extended beyond the classroom to their colleagues and the broader community in which they worked, and continued to be an essential driver of their sense of professionalism.

5

NAVIGATING THE STORM

Occupational and subjective wellbeing

Introduction

> We all just feel like we're on our own, trying to keep our heads above water, and no one's coming to save us.
>
> *(Zoe, secondary, early, Interview 5)*

Teachers often use metaphor to make sense of their experiences and professional identities (Thomas & Beauchamp, 2011). We might, therefore, consider how teaching during a pandemic can be likened to teachers finding the strength and skills to navigate their way through a relentless storm that buffeted them in different directions, at times blowing them off course and threatening to drown them.

> I think the biggest challenge is that everything doesn't seem normal. It almost feels like we're just living in this book and the story hasn't ended yet...
>
> *(Samantha, primary, middle, Interview 1)*

As Samantha described, teaching during the pandemic felt to her like living in a work of fiction as it was not a 'normal' experience. If we combine this idea with the metaphor of steering a ship, we might think of Samantha's story being like 'The Odyssey' where the main character's commitment and resourcefulness, combined with support from others, enables him to overcome sustained suffering and setbacks. Yet there can be little doubt that retaining the hearts and minds of experienced teachers, 'is challenged by work-related ill health...[which is]...often associated with poor psychosocial work conditions (Björk et al., 2019, p. 956).

DOI: 10.4324/9781003391661-5

54 Navigating the storm

Relatively little research has followed teachers over time as they managed and were assisted in managing their sense of wellbeing through the challenges experienced during the COVID-19 pandemic. Many studies have focussed on the negative effects of the pandemic period on teachers' wellbeing which have resulted in, according to one independent UK annual survey of 3,000 teachers, 78% of all staff experiencing mental health symptoms due to their work, with 72% feeling stressed and 54% considering leaving teaching due to pressures on their wellbeing (Education Support, 2022). Yet teachers' stories revealed a different picture. Certainly, the teachers in this research experienced these challenges as uncertainties, and changes to their normal ways of working continued to disrupt individual teachers and pupils' health and wellbeing. However, the evidence from this research provides more nuanced, and primarily positive perspectives, capturing the teachers' voices as they spoke of their own fluctuating sense of subjective wellbeing over the two-year research period.

The chapter illustrates how teachers managed to keep their heads above water as they steered the storm's surging waves or, to use another metaphor, rode what one teacher called the 'rollercoaster' of the pandemic. It shows how almost all the teachers managed to navigate their way through the early shocks and on-going perturbations, drawing upon personal, professional and social school-related resources to maintain their sense of professional purpose and capabilities, and sustain their commitment to teaching and their current school. The chapter is divided into three parts: i) the meanings of 'wellbeing'; ii) fluctuations: coping with uncertainty as teachers managed their frustrations, fears, and fatigue; and iii) strengthening commitment and wellbeing: how almost all the teachers survived the early shocks and on-going perturbations by drawing upon personal, professional and social resources to strengthen their deep sense of professionalism.

Meanings of wellbeing

Two kinds of wellbeing have been identified. The first, 'occupational wellbeing' has been defined as 'teachers' responses to the cognitive, emotional, health and social conditions pertaining to their work and profession'; and the second, 'subjective wellbeing', has been defined as 'teachers' self-reported experiences and assessment of the quality of their working lives and the sense of purpose and capabilities that they need to live a happy and fulfilling life as a teacher' (OECD, 2020, p.18). A broader, more encompassing definition of wellbeing that acknowledges the presence of the personal in the professional, and the interaction between these is, however, more reflective of what teachers in this project reported. Diener and his colleagues defined subjective wellbeing as 'reflecting an overall evaluation of the quality of a person's life from his or her perspective … The extent to which a person believes or feels that his or her own life is going well' (Diener et al., 2018, p. 1). They found that a key predictor of subjective wellbeing is social relationships, and that higher subjective wellbeing, 'is associated with good health and longevity, better social relationships, work performance and creativity' (Diener et al., 2018, p. i). The interdependence of the occupational and the personal captures well the ongoing integration in their work, and the ways in which their personal and professional lives are interwoven in defining the essence of what being professional means. This has been reinforced by research showing that teachers' mental health can be supported by school-related individual and collective interventions which reduce excessive worrying, depressive and anxiety symptoms (Dray et al., 2017), and decrease the potential for depersonalisation through enforced periods of isolation from colleagues and pupils that might otherwise affect teachers' belief in their ability to provide quality education and thus pupil progress and achievement (Bandura, 1997; Zee & Koomen, 2016). More recently, Song and his colleagues added 'quality', 'purpose' and 'capability' in defining the wellbeing of teachers specifically: 'teachers' self-reported experience and assessment of the quality of their working lives and the sense of purpose and capabilities that they need to lead a happy and fulfilling life as a teacher' (Song et al., 2020, p. 6), identifying altruism, moral purpose, and job satisfaction as important indicators. Soini et al. (2010) identified four inter-dependent aspects of teacher wellbeing: i) interaction with students; ii) interaction with colleagues; iii) making evaluations; and iv) choosing and developing instructional tools. Arguably, each of these was under threat as the pandemic continued to disrupt norms of teaching and learning, disrupting the kinds of interaction with students upon which teachers historically depend for their own sense of competent professionalism, self-esteem and achievement. Finally, in perhaps the most expansive definition of subjective wellbeing, Seligman (2012) defines the construct as an amalgam of: positive emotion (the subjective measure of happiness and life satisfaction); positive engagement (with the task); positive social relationships (sense of belonging, being supported); and vocation (serving something which you believe is bigger than yourself in importance).

The next part of this chapter illustrates the many fears, anxieties and stresses experienced at different times during the teachers' personal and professional journeys during its early phase as the pandemic disrupted their lives and work. At the same time, it illustrates how this was followed by a (sometimes uncertain) recovery phase during which, although their sense of wellbeing continued to be sorely tested, most kept their heads above water, drawing on personal and professional resources to steer their way through, reconfirming their commitment to themselves and others.

Fluctuations: coping with uncertainty

One of the most consistently felt adversities of the pandemic was the uncertainty. Most teachers associated the initial lockdown and/ or the return to

56 Navigating the storm

school after the first partial closure with the unknown, strangeness and lack of normality. This created feelings of anxiety, worry and even fear for many.

> It was kind of a mixture, which I think is why it was so hard … you're trying to negotiate your way through different situations that come up at different times.
>
> *(Lucy, primary, early, Interview 3)*

> It's been like a rollercoaster – it's so up and down. Even like in a day, it's so up and down…It's just that constant uncertainty of what's going to come next? Are we going to teaching online again? Are lots of pupils going to be off? Do we need to be doing teaching on Teams at the same time as teaching a lesson? Are we going to have staff absences? There's all of that constantly in the back of your mind, and it feels like you can't really plan too far in advance.
>
> *(Mia, secondary, early, Interview 4)*

> Sometimes I sit in the classroom and I think 'is this ever going to be the same?' Before, you would walk in, you would have a full class of children and if a child fell might your first initial reaction is to run and go and hug, and now it's um. Yes, we have to think twice. This is really hard, and I think we all have a similar feeling. It is scary. It's not nice….I feel very anxious and nervous initially when I get into the building, but as soon as I see the teachers and the staff, I'm fine. And then reality hits when you leave the classroom. 'Oh gosh, I have been with so many children. Am I carrying something? I'm going to go home. Am I going to?' It's that worry in the back off your mind…And then also just worrying. Yeah, just worrying about things that you would never worry about before. But I think we've got used to it a little bit.
>
> *(Samantha, primary, middle, Interview 1)*

However, as time went on Samantha became less worried by the situation which had become part of everyday life, and shifted her focus to what she thought was best for her pupils.

> The only thing that came up in the news the other day was about the coming September when the children are going back to school. It's going to be completely normal. Some of them will be vaccinated, some of them are not going to be vaccinated, but everything is going to be running back to normal… That does scare me a little bit, because right now we are doing COVID guidelines. We are following guidelines, and they are saying in the news that there is no expectation really to do that anymore because they're saying lots of people have been vaccinated and some of them haven't. But you just have to. It's just going to be. It's going to be

normal. Before, I used to panic a little bit ...[but] ...I'm not fazed now. I think we've learned to deal with it. It's become everyday life. I feel drained. I'm very tired and but I'm OK like nothing is affecting me.... You just have to get through it. You just have to keep going. Keep going, the more we stick to routine, the better it is for our children.

(Samantha, primary, middle, Interview 3)

Managing workload

Increasing and uncertain workloads made it difficult for some teachers to keep their heads above water and manage their wellbeing.

Barbara described how exhausted she felt with having to live and work in different ways whilst also feeling the pressure to ensure her pupils were making academic progress.

I feel absolutely exhausted because when you plan lessons in a classroom, it's so different than planning online. I love to travel. I feel a bit trapped. I'm a very 'choice' person...there's a massive difference between a choice and a decision...the choice is something within you and you take a stand for that. So that aspect of not being able to travel...not being able to see people. The teaching side of it is a joy – it's everything else that comes along with it. People have lost people during Covid, some people are experiencing Long Covid – they have families – nothing of that is taken into account, it's more, more, more, more, so we can tick boxes for when Ofsted comes in.

(Barbara, secondary, middle, Interview 1)

I think we might see a bit of a surge in people going off sick. Some people are hanging on by a thread...I feel absolutely exhausted... I really miss the times when wellbeing was actually a word that meant something. It's like the word 'surreal' is used all the time, and incorrectly so many times, and what it represented was such a great word, and now I think that that's what wellbeing has become. It's just 'oh the students' wellbeing, we're concerned about your wellbeing' – and there is no wellbeing. And I think we feel unappreciated, run down, nothing we do is good enough.

(Barbara, secondary, middle, Interview 2)

These challenges had an impact on her professional identity and more specifically her self-efficacy.

It makes me question am I not a good teacher? Am I not doing enough? You can see on everybody's faces – we can't be doing any more than we

58 Navigating the storm

> are. I love being back in the classroom. I'm happy, the kids were happy... They drive me crazy, but they're so onboard most of them, and I absolutely love teaching them – it's fun, they can have a laugh, they make fun of each other in a lovely way, they ask questions. I will say that of all the kids that I've taught when we were in lockdown, that class was the most responsive. I am so worried, because I don't have the training to be able help these kids. I can differentiate till the cows come home – that's fine – but in terms of that, I'm not qualified, it's not my expertise. I've asked for help. I'm tired in my bones. Mental health wise I feel fine, I'm just very tired, disappointed, but just get on with it.
>
> *(Barbara, secondary, middle, Interview 2)*

Two early-phase teachers expressed similar sentiments.

> I did at one point feel completely overwhelmed about my workload and having to manage subject leadership, school-wide projects, teaching at school and online, marking at school and online, calling parents, dealing with conflicts, supporting disadvantaged, encouraging more online participation, dealing with Covid in the family and trying to maintain my own mental health. I had many plates spinning at the same time...I have not stopped once. We had to keep going. We had no choice really, but I felt like giving up many times. It was really hard.
>
> *(Lucy, primary, early, Journal 2)*

Mia described having 'had a headache every evening from staring at the screen marking for so long (teams auto marking feature is a big help). There isn't much else to this week' (Journal 2).

For teachers with parents, working from home brought other challenges. Natalie commented,

> It was quite tough to suddenly be at home, and then trying to balance – I'm not very good at balancing work life balance anyway, but even more so when you're at home, and I've got two girls, who were then at home, and then my partner's working from home, and it's all a bit much!
>
> *(Natalie, secondary, middle, Interview 1)*

Kath found it difficult being a single parent but had shown resilience by getting on with things, working in the evenings when her son was in bed, and putting others' needs before herself. However, she resolved to start looking after her wellbeing more, and asking others for help.

In contrast, Sandra was able to prioritise her wellbeing when working from home.

You know what you can do and what you can't do, so you work within that and go for a walk with the dog, if the weather's quite nice you go sit in the garden – you make the best of what you can do. That for me is what's kept me going. In the 1st lockdown I decided to lose weight and I succeeded. I now make sure there's an hour where I can go for a walk, swimming and running. I used to be one of those people who worked till 11pm but realised that once you stop putting that pressure on yourself its easier.

(Sandra, secondary, later, Interview 2)

Anna, a secondary school teacher, felt emotionally drained when her school re-opened to all pupils with little time to prepare. She thought that staff wellbeing, which had been better in previous terms, had been eroded by the expectations of senior leaders, who also failed to recognise the impact of these expectations on her wellbeing. However, by clinging to other staff and pulling together, she was able to keep going.

> In terms of staff wellbeing and staff mental health and staff care, we could have had a week to just get our heads round the idea of what we were being asked to do, to get our heads around and hearts around the emotional aspect of what we were going through as well. But I felt very much like I was a cog in a machine in that first week back, because we were thrown into it straightaway.
>
> *(Anna, secondary, early, Interview 1)*

> Teachers are clinging onto each other and we're clinging on by a thread, some more than others at the moment... Staff morale and staff mental health are, at the moment, at the lowest that I've seen them all year. Absolute lowest. People are tired, people are worried.
>
> *(Anna, secondary, early, Interview 3)*

> I think there was a sense of pulling together and rallying and knowing what needed to be done... The general frustration of feeling, in terms of morale, feeling like we have been working really, really hard for two years to make sure the schools stay open, that the kids stay safe. We've adapted in so many different ways, with technology in the classroom, with making sure we've got live lessons set up online, with making sure that kids don't miss out on work if they need to self-isolate. And there doesn't seem to be any, from anywhere... any recognition... No one seems to get it. And no one seems to be saying 'God, you had it hard, haven't you? It's been really rough'.
>
> *(Anna, secondary, early, Interview 4)*

60 Navigating the storm

Like Anna, a positive school culture and strong relationships with her colleagues were important for Marion, Sandra and Sara's wellbeing.

> There's lot of people that if you're feeling stressed or you want to just offload, that will listen. We're all kind of caring of each other. It's quite a supportive staff. There aren't the cliquey groups where nobody talks to anybody else – we are just one big staff.
>
> *(Marion, secondary, middle, Interview 2)*

> In school, SLT have been more prone to celebrating good things going on, so feel more valued, which has helped. School has changed, become more supportive and caring towards members of staff. People are being more open and honest about their feelings e.g., if I have a bad day, other people are more accepting of it, supporting them.
>
> *(Sandra, secondary, later, Interview 4)*

> School does a lot with wellbeing e.g. Wellbeing Wednesdays where we get a PowerPoint slide with quotes… [however]… the school is continuing to operate how it was in the pandemic.
>
> *(Sara, primary, later, Interview 3)*

Max, a secondary teacher, felt that the impact on his wellbeing of having to manage a heavy workload alongside fears for his and his partner's health had not been recognised by schools. His partner had tested positive for COVID-19 during her half term break which required Max

> to self-isolate three days before I was due to break up and for the entirety of my half term. This was an unsettling period for both of us since we were both worried about the impact of the virus on my partner's health. There was little recognition from my workplace at the mental strains this placed on both of us and for the week leading up to half-term when I was isolating and awaiting a test, the workload remained consistently demanding … Thankfully my partner made a quick recovery but the mental impact of losing the half-term to isolation significantly affected our return to school after the break, with both of us suffering from high levels of anxiety and questioning if we should consider staying in the profession.
>
> *(Max, secondary, early, Journal 1)*

Zoe, another secondary teacher, spoke of her 'inner battles' with depression and anxiety for which she took medication. Having training cut short, then going into a department of one in the middle of pandemic created a lot of panic for her.

It used to be that I would get home at sixish, then go to bed at 8pm. It was like come home, shove some food in your face, and then go to bed, which was really miserable.

(Zoe, secondary, early, Interview 5)

However, she made the decision to move to accommodation closer to her school, giving her more time to herself in the evening and the ability to stay after school later as she had less of a commute, allowing her to better manage her work and life.

For some, there were 'dips' as a result of unexpected increases in workload as schools fully reopened after lockdowns and responded to external demands for an increase in pupils' academic progress and achievement.

The bombshell was then dropped that all middle leaders were to write up a 'Curriculum Intent' document to explain the curriculum choices regarding sequencing and content to 'external audiences' and our entire curriculum 'journey' from years 7 to 11 was to be 'written up' in a consistent format across the school to be uploaded to the school's website. My heart sank through the floor, and I felt more despondent than I have throughout the entire pandemic. Truly. For any subject this would be a huge piece of work, but for a core subject it is enormous. I cannot fathom how many hours this would take to complete and undoubtedly it would have to be shared out amongst the rest of the team. And it would likely take up all of our 'Development Time' for the rest of the year. And for what?! This will have precisely ZERO impact on progress of students or the quality of teaching and learning in the department, or the professional development of staff. It is just a gigantic waste of time! Nobody outside the department needs that information and to waste a year's worth of staff time just to tick a box for Ofsted is criminal in my opinion. I haven't spent a single minute on this work since, and do not intend to. Unfortunately, I see this as just the first step back to the worst of what we experienced before the pandemic. This is a significant factor in me actively looking for another profession, which is a shame, as so many good teachers will leave for this type of reason... The changes of policies, some of the stupid things that they've thought of or suggested, or the lack of warning on things, is frustrating – but that's not just been about Covid. Many, many governments have made many, many stupid decisions about education, and I've felt equally frustrated.

(Neil, secondary, middle, Journal 4)

Mia reported that,

We've all got those strategies that we use – go to the gym, or go for a walk or whatever it is. At the moment, a lot of those aren't available.

62 Navigating the storm

When I get home, I need to be planning. Normally I'd be really strict with myself, I say 'okay, I'm going to do two hours of work because then I'm going to the gym, or whatever', but now I can't. It's easy to stare at my laptop for four hours.

(Mia, secondary, early, Interview 4)

Struggles with managing the added workload of the twin focus on pupils' wellbeing and academic progress, which continued to be disrupted by health-related absences, caused only one teacher to leave classroom teaching.

Cate, a primary school teacher, had been struggling with her wellbeing since before the pandemic. She was feeling 'tired and overworked' (Interview 2). Due to moving classrooms and getting it ready for September, she 'didn't have much of a summer' (Interview 4). She had also stopped socialising with colleagues because 'I've been trying to manage my time. So sadly, I've not really seen much of my colleagues' (Interview 4). She calculated that she was working around 52 hours a week.

> I do have a bit of a reputation for being here the longest, but I try my best not to take as much home with me. I don't ever take books home with me, that's for sure. We've got all the pressures again of the data handling and making sure the books are marked, and it's all piled on again. So, because you're holding onto all that stress inside your head, it doesn't take as much to knock you over the edge.
>
> *(Cate, primary, early, Interview 4)*

> It has been a struggle, and I have made myself unwell. I have had violent and aggressive language and behaviour towards myself and other children on a regular basis and have felt unheard and unsupported on the matter. There's a child that needs extra one-to-one support for their own – and others' – sake. Originally, I was offered no extra adult at all. It's been a constant battle between making phone calls for emergency support and spending 100% of my energy trying to de-escalate high-level behaviour. For a few weeks, I had a spare teaching assistant (TA) that would come and support me when his other one-to-one support wasn't here: he often did it off his own back though, and just came to me when he was free, as he knew that I was struggling. I keep getting told that we just don't have the funds for more support. I understand that is an issue, but so is the learning, enjoyment and safety of the rest of the children. I have voiced my concern numerous times. I don't know how I'm going to get through. I want more than anything to make their final year a memorable and happy one for all of us.
>
> *(Cate, primary, early, Journal 5)*

The problem is, each year, more boxes keep being added and nothing gets taken away. All these boxes aren't boxes that have made me a better teacher, they're preventing me from being my best, they're just taking up my time and effectively making me a stressed, therefore worse, teacher. I'm not just mad at the system and everyone involved, what's worse is that I'm mad at myself. I know I could try to make changes, and I'm not doing anything to fight it, I'm just continuing to tick my boxes. Who is going to take accountability for these problems with the system? Maybe the government don't even know the extent of the problem, how can they when we just continue with our fake smiling faces? Spouting off about how rewarding it is to teach children (it really is) and neglecting to mention the reality of teaching, the hours and hours of work outside the classroom. I can't continue to be part of this.

(Cate, primary, early, Journal 5)

Cate left the school at the end of the year but remained in education.

Strengthening commitment and wellbeing

The overwhelming number of teachers were not only able to find ways to navigate their way through, but, by 'facing the storm', had also been able to strengthen their commitment and enthusiasm for their work.

Michelle asserted that her commitment had not decreased despite describing extreme tiredness at the start of the pandemic.

I am personally going through tiredness I can't remember feeling for a long time, and I think that's purely because of the length that we've been in this situation and also the number of people around us that we need to care for.

(Michelle, primary, later, Interview 1)

In her fifth interview she described how teaching during the pandemic had given her a renewed sense of purpose and responsibility, which boosted her confidence and commitment.

It's perhaps brought about a sense of purpose that my eyes weren't as open to before. I'm a teacher and therefore we understand children, but because the pandemic opened my eyes more to perhaps their home circumstances, their family circumstances, their community circumstances in which they live whenever they're not at school. So, I suppose it's possibly broadened. Or really made me rethink about something that I already knew but made me think about it in a different way. So from that point of view, when I'm standing in front of

64 Navigating the storm

my class, I'm probably just wanting to give them even slightly more, beyond the academic, the social connection, the emotional connection, that stability. And unrelated, of course to pandemic, but even more so now to do with what they're here to do with the war in Ukraine as well. It's another thing that the children need to help have unpicked, at their level. So I feel that sense of responsibility. So, I think that's the drive that keeps me as committed, especially when other colleagues, either on the same level as you or superior, actually say 'look, you're doing this really well or I'm going to send this person to you because you can help them with that.' So, there are times where your confidence is boosted. It's been that broadening of, uhm, my consciousness if you like, in terms of being more aware of what some of our children go home to at night. That has been the way that I've changed. And that will have always been there, but it's probably more at the forefront of my consciousness now, and my responsibility too.

(Michelle, primary, later, Interview 5)

Lucy was initially worried that she would catch COVID-19 at school and pass it on.

> Every time I come into work that's what I think about on the way to work. I think about it when the children are in the classroom. I think about it every day.
>
> *(Lucy, primary, early, Interview 1)*

Lucy described feeling a huge sense of responsibility and risk and being 'on the edge all the time' (Interview 1). She explained that a few months into the first lockdown her

> mental health was really bad and the worst I've ever been. I do suffer occasionally... but it was low, to the point where I had to seek out help for it... I was struggling to do anything in the day... It was just everything was just so painful.
>
> *(Lucy, primary, early, Interview 1)*

Yet Lucy also felt that being with the children provided a distraction and enjoyed being back in school after the first lockdown when she had had to work solely from home. 'Being extremely anxious all the time is one of the biggest challenges for me and trying to relieve that anxiety in little ways as I can is really important. The children do a lot of that for me... but it's still there' (Interview 1).

Lucy spoke of her commitment to her work became even stronger as she faced up to and overcame various challenges.

> Now my commitment might be stronger because I know how much the children need us, considering during the pandemic they didn't have us for extended periods of time. And we saw the repercussions of that. I think it's made me more committed to ensuring that they have the best outcomes. I think my motivation has stayed the same. That's not to say that sometimes within the pandemic itself, there were times when it did dip....but I've seen how much teachers provide for the children. I know that I support the children with, not only their academic abilities, but also with their emotional wellbeing. That gives me confidence because I know the outcomes of my work. So, I knew that what I do has a positive impact on the children and that gives me confidence to keep going and to do it. I think we were put in a situation where we had to keep going, not give up, and then how many challenges was set against us. So that means that my resilience has probably been tested more....[but]... having been through the pandemic ...I think I'm more resilient. I think it's been tested, but it's been made stronger. I think that the way that other people have reacted towards teachers during the pandemic, on the way that the pressure has been mounted upon schools, has changed my view of me as a professional a little bit. It's made me feel a bit like we're not as important or as influential as we actually are, if you see what I mean. Because we see the children every day, we are there to see every sort of change that happens to them, and that puts us in a really powerful position as major players in their life. I think if anything I strive more to ensure that those relationships are really solid with them, and I think that's probably what the pandemic is giving me. It's really valuing my job and how important my job is, and therefore every little thing I do, every minute I spend is well worthwhile, you know. You're going to have meaningful moments with them.
>
> *(Lucy, primary, early, Interview 5)*

Similar to Lucy, Grace spoke of gains for her wellbeing and commitment through focusing on her pupils' needs.

> I get my energy from being at work...from some children. It might be that there are mental health issues, not necessarily you know, for all children. For some children it might be that you know they're not able to attend schools. Still, parents are saying that they've got Covid and things like that, so it's really important that we are really focused and really committed... I think it's increased in some ways because actually I think it's really important that we plug those gaps.
>
> *(Grace, primary, middle, Interview 5)*

66 Navigating the storm

For Margaret government changes in teaching (e.g., online teaching), workload and managing mental health of colleagues seemed to be her biggest challenges throughout pandemic. Nevertheless, she was able to maintain her commitment by separating work from home and focusing on her sense of purpose.

> So, I think the biggest challenge actually was not managing it for the children. We had a lot of anxious staff who have vulnerable people living at home... Emotions were the hardest thing that I've had to deal with since September. I just try and make school, school, and home, home. So when I'm in school I'm in work mode and I think about work, and then when I'm at home I try and not think about work and just do really nice home things... And I think that helps with my resilience. There have been times when I would happily hand over the role that I'm in at the minute, but I think that's just because it's testing on my emotions and patience and workload. But then I think you just you do it for the children. So since coming back, it's actually better because at home you are almost overcompensating for not being at school. I've absolutely loved being back at school I mean, I really enjoy it. I was dreading the home learning but then I really enjoyed it. For my own mental health and wellbeing it was a challenge. But I think it was good. It meant I learned to be more resilient.
>
> *(Margaret, primary, middle, Interview 4)*

Like Margaret, overcoming new challenges was empowering for Fern. Although she was in her final years of teaching, she saw the pandemic as bringing her amazing, 'unbelievable' challenges that reaffirmed her teaching skills.

> For the most part, the challenge was exciting, so that you were totally thinking outside for the box. People would look back at this time and think I can't believe what I did before. It helped me through the pandemic having the challenge and needing to go to school each day, but equally I am becoming reflective on whether I could have stayed motivated longer if I had had the balance in my life [being able to get away, see family]. I think it proved that you have a number of differing skills, that you probably knew you had, but had never been pushed or had a reason to be challenged.
>
> *(Fern, primary, later, Interview 5)*

Teresa spoke of her continuing dedication.

> The level of commitment hasn't gone down, definitely, and I'm probably even more determined than ever to try and get things right

for the children. And I think yeah, everything has gone on you, just you feel like some somebody needs to have their backs, if that makes sense. So I say, yeah, I think I'm definitely feeling more, 'I want to do this for the children and get it right for them'. And I think we've almost had a chance to look at how we do things and possibly adapt things and change things. And we need to use that as an opportunity rather than as a barrier. I think one thing that's come out of the whole pandemic is the need to have more of a work life balance. Which is possibly something that we didn't see before, but because of the pandemic, we did have more time for ourselves. It's made those things really clear. So although I'm just as motivated to work as hard as I always have done, I'm also making sure that I have time for myself as well. I think it's made us all become more resilient ... I think I'm a better leader than I was before. I think I am a better, better deputy head than I was before. I think I've learned a lot about leading schools and how to manage people and support people throughout this.

(Teresa, primary, middle, Interview 5)

Conclusion

As we have seen from earlier chapters in this book, teachers needed to draw upon and develop new personal and material resources, learn new skills and provide sustained focus upon pupil welfare and wellbeing as well as academic learning in order to continue to 'make a difference', whilst also maintaining their own welfare and wellbeing. Wellbeing at work is important because there are relationships between this and teachers' perceived self-efficacy, motivation, engagement and their classroom effectiveness (McCallum & Price, 2010; Owen, 2016; Soini et al., 2010; Lyubomirsky et al., 2005; Garbett & Thomas, 2020). Individuals are likely to use different weightings to determine their subjective sense of wellbeing (Diener et al, 2018) and, as we have illustrated in this chapter, these will relate to their own biographies, lives outside their school settings, as well as within them. Nevertheless, common patterns of influence on wellbeing have been identified. Broadly, these can be classified as being related to their psychological and social capital – teachers' sense of vocation, and the strength of individual, social and resource support received in the school – as they managed the turbulence and perturbations of the pandemic, and the challenges that these brought to physical and mental health and teaching and learning.

Teachers in this project were clear that sustaining their personal (subjective) sense of wellbeing was fundamental to their ability to be caring, resilient and effective in their workplaces. Contrary to largely negative reports on the state of teacher wellbeing during and after the pandemic period, as we have shown in this and earlier chapters, the levels of care, commitment and wellbeing of these teachers remained high; and although almost all teachers emerged tired their sense of wellbeing was intact.

6

PROFESSIONAL IDENTITIES

The importance of agency

Introduction

Teachers' professional identities (how they see themselves in the workplace) matter. The pandemic shone a light on care within teacher identity, intensifying its importance for teachers in knowing and understanding 'how to be', and 'how to act' and 'how to understand their work' (Sachs, 2005, p. 15) as a teacher. As observed long ago, 'it matters to teachers themselves, as well as to their pupils, who and what they are' (Nias, 1989, pp. 202–203, cited in Kelchtermans, 2009).

This identification of the person in the professional is an important observation, since it explains both the core service ethic which pervades many teachers' views of their purposes, and the care which characterises their relationships with pupils. Together, they provide a door way to understanding how, if these are threatened, so too might their willingness and ability to teach to their best (Day, 2017). The pandemic also highlighted the importance of self-efficacy (Bandura, 1997) and context-in-action (Priestley et al., 2016) for teacher agency.

Yet, 'teacher identity is not something that is fixed nor is it imposed; rather it is negotiated through experience and the sense that is made of that experience' (Sachs, 2005, p. 15). A range of research has demonstrated that teachers' identities are not, and cannot be, guaranteed always to be stable over a career. They evolve and fluctuate over their career in response to changing personal, social, cultural, political, and historical forces: their relationships with others, their perceptions of self, and their different experiences within and outside the workplace (see Burke & Stets, 2009; Day et al., 2006, 2007; Rodgers & Scott, 2008; Stryker et al., 2005); and how they manage the interface between these.

DOI: 10.4324/9781003391661-6

70 Professional identities

Unsurprisingly, the onset and spread of COVID-19 impacted how teachers constructed their ideas of 'how to be', 'how to understand' and how to enact their work. For the teachers in our study, the pandemic created additional challenges and experiences, raising levels of professional unease and distress (Stets & Osborn, 2008), affecting their relationships with others, sense of self, and confidence in their ability to teach to their best. The pandemic also meant teachers questioning and re-assessing their roles and relationships with others which, in some cases, led them to secure a stronger sense of professional identity.

The chapter begins by considering how self-efficacy and agency shaped these teachers' identities. It then examines the emotional nature of teachers' work during the pandemic, recognising how emotions influenced the way teachers understood their role. Finally, it considers how teachers' feelings towards and experiences with pupils they considered to be 'disadvantaged' played a significant part in the formation of their professional identities.

Self-efficacy and agency

Teacher self-efficacy requires a belief that one can positively influence pupil outcomes (Corry & Stella, 2018) which then shapes the actions teachers do or do not choose to take, the amount of effort and time they invest in their chosen actions and, depending on whether they achieve their desired outcomes, their sense of achievement. Personal efficacy is a key factor in influencing human agency, for 'If people believe they have no power to produce results, they will not attempt to make things happen' (Bandura, 1997, p. 3); and agency itself 'should not be understood as an individual capacity – as something that individuals have or don't have – but as something that is achieved in and through concrete contexts-for-action' (Priestley et al., 2016, p. 34).

Drawing on Taylor's (1977) definition of agency, Edwards (2015) states that,

> To be agentic we need to be able to make responsible strong judgements about the worth of our intentions when we take actions. Also, we need to be able to evaluate for ourselves whether we have met the goals we have set ourselves.
>
> *(Edwards, 2015, p. 780)*

Research suggests that teacher agency is not something that teachers *have* but is something they *do*, as a result of the interplay between their individual capacities and the contexts in which they work. Thus, it is important, when trying to understand teacher agency, to examine the cultures and relationships that shape teachers' beliefs in their ability to achieve their goals and, in turn, the actions they choose to take.

It is, therefore, also important to acknowledge that teacher agency is likely to fluctuate over time as contexts change. The authors argue that contexts include not just a teacher's past personal and professional experiences, the educational aims of their school as well as their wider values, ambitions and beliefs, but also the immediate context of a specific situation, how the teacher assesses the situation to decide on possible actions and the resources available to them. These resources include how teachers think and talk about a situation (both to themselves and with others), the physical environment and the relationships they have with others. Thus, we can view teacher agency as influenced by, and part of, varying contexts-for-action which include teachers' sense of self-efficacy.

The remainder of this section examines the extent to which the contexts in which teachers found themselves working during the pandemic enabled agentic action and supported their sense of self-efficacy, and how their professional identities were reinforced or threatened as a consequence.

Self-efficacy doubts

> I had a lot of inner battles of, well, you didn't get your full training year so how are you expecting to do this? You can't do it, why are you doing it?
>
> *(Zoe, secondary, early, Interview 1)*

Teaching in the context of a pandemic meant teachers having to act in different and, often, untried ways. For example, creating online content, teaching remotely and managing different classroom configurations. However, these actions were often enforced and unavoidable (rather than chosen) due to COVID-19 restrictions and leadership decisions, threatening some teachers' sense of self-efficacy and professional identity.

Most of the 12 early-phase teachers, whose teacher identities were not yet fully formed (Beauchamp & Thomas, 2009), experienced feelings of self-doubt and uncertainty due to disrupted teacher preparation programmes, restricted professional development opportunities and having to adapt to quickly changing situations (see Chapter 2). In the early months of the pandemic, Mia, Anna, Cate, Zoe, Patricia and Lucy (a mix of primary and secondary teachers) described feeling 'powerless' and 'like an imposter', wondering if they were doing things correctly, letting pupils down and questioning their professional decisions. These feelings were compounded by their ability to act being restricted, showing how teachers' sense of self-efficacy influences, and is influenced by, teacher agency (Bandura, 1997).

> I found it very challenging to support them [pupils] using our behaviour techniques from a distance (owing to Covid safety measures) as usually I would have a private conversation with them. As this student left the classroom, they swore at me which led to an exclusion. I feel that in normal circumstances it would have been easier to diffuse the situation

using the school's behaviour techniques which may have prevented this outcome. This was a really challenging situation for me and I was quite upset by the outcome as I felt I had let the student down.

(Mia, secondary, early, Journal 2)

I feel like I am unable to do my job effectively, as I am not able to provide that support to quieter students who often wait for me to be close to them before they ask me questions, so they don't have to call out in front of the rest of the class. This aspect makes me feel like I am starting to fail as a teacher. It is also starting to have an impact on my confidence.

(Patricia, secondary, early, Journal 1)

These examples demonstrate Priestley et al.'s (2016) notion of teacher agency as arising from the interplay between teachers' individual capacities and the contexts in which they work. Contexts, which included adapting to new ways of teaching and school restrictions, made it more difficult for these teachers to achieve the outcomes they desired for their pupils, reducing their sense of self-efficacy and opportunities for agentic action.

It was not just early-phase teachers who doubted their abilities in the earlier stages of the pandemic as they found themselves working in contexts they had not experienced before, and for which they had no training. Neil (secondary, middle) commented that having to find new ways of teaching pupils who were working from home had 'made a lot of experienced staff feel like beginning teachers again' (Interview 3). Finding that their years of classroom teaching experience had not prepared them for teaching during a pandemic, led to three middle-phase teachers (Orla, Barbara and Emma) feeling vulnerable as they questioned their self-efficacy and professional identity. Orla (secondary) commented that she had 'times when I really doubt, you know, exactly how good I am in the classroom. Am I right here in my assessments of students' work, am I not?... I felt a lot more unsure and uncertain' (Interview 2). Barbara (secondary) also questioned whether she was a good teacher when struggling to get completed work back from pupils who were not in school. Meanwhile, Emma (primary) was anxious about returning to teach in school after an extended period of working from home where she had been isolated from her colleagues due to her 'clinically vulnerable' status. Emma described feeling 'a bit deskilled'. She felt, 'like the new girl starting all over again.... I've stood still and the world's kept moving' (Interview 2).

As a professional, I'm a bit worried about going back because I haven't taught for three months and really teaching experience over the last year is numbered in weeks. That's going to be quite difficult ... just walking into a classroom and doing the job that I'm trained for.

(Emma, primary, middle, Interview 2)

Her sense of professional identity was damaged further when her subject leader role in the school was given to another member of staff (Journal 1).

Building self-efficacy through action

For three teachers (Anna, Lucy and Neil), the pandemic offered possibilities to take mindful, intentional action to support their pupils' learning. As a result of self-reflection and persistence, they were able to act in ways that supported successful outcomes for their pupils and colleagues, boosting their sense of self-efficacy and professional identities,

After initially struggling with doubts that her blended teaching approach was not positively impacting her pupils' learning, Anna (secondary, early) adapted her teaching to allow for more 'curiosity-driven' learning. Seeing the positive impact of her actions on her pupils' engagement and learning, restored Anna's sense of confidence and strengthened a professional identity based on doing what she believed to be best for her pupils. She commented that if she ever got 'to the point when this job doesn't bring me joy, or I can't be the real me, then I need to find something else to do' (Interview 1). For Anna, feeling empowered to act according to what she believed was in her pupils' best interests was an important element of her professional identity. Anna's example suggests that, for some teachers, feeling vulnerable and having self-efficacy doubts can provide a context for growth and teacher agency, as they offer an opportunity for reflection, learning and improvement (Bullough, 2005; Wheatley, 2002).

Lucy chose to focus on pupils' individual learning needs and repeatedly practising key skills rather than trying to keep up with curriculum expectations. She felt that her actions enabled most of her pupils to make good progress after the lockdown, to feel positive about their learning and happy to be in school. As Lucy continued to act in ways that she felt positively impacted her pupils, her sense of self-efficacy was strengthened, so that by the fifth interview she had developed confidence in her actions and a commitment to her work.

> I knew I had a positive impact on the children and that gives me the confidence to keep going and to do it. And that comes from experience of teaching children quite a lot and having a couple of classes. And it comes from seeing the children take massive steps in their progress. My confidence builds when they are successful.
>
> *(Lucy, primary, early, Interview 5)*

Neil, at the start of the pandemic, found himself responsible for making decisions around how to adapt the teaching of his specialist subject for pupils who were learning at home. Like Anna and Lucy, he chose an approach that produced successful outcomes for both pupils and colleagues.

74 Professional identities

> I feel I have done a really good job with… remote provision and this blended approach to learning and everything that had to go along with it. Because I took a decision very early on to do quite a centralised, streamlined approach across the whole department, which was fairly novel. I think, on my part, without blowing my own trumpet, it showed a pretty good level of foresight for how challenging it might be delivering an alternative. And all my other colleagues, actually in every other department, have gone down the different route, which was actually the one that was kind of imposed by senior leaders. I kind of went a bit off-piste and did my own thing and I'd kind of kept it covertly a little bit quiet until it was kind of done. And then they let me roll with it and we agreed to let it play out and it was ultimately fairly successful. But I wouldn't say it's massively more successful than what other departments have, but it's just been a hell of a lot easier for us to do.
>
> *(Neil, secondary, middle, Interview 4)*

As well as being well-received by his colleagues who appreciated a more manageable workload than colleagues in other departments, pupils' attainment had not suffered.

> It was a very pleasant surprise when I actually analysed that data. It kind of goes against what some people are saying in terms of this national recovery effort and having to catch up and how much, how many months of progress students are behind. I don't see it in my school for our subject.
>
> *(Neil, secondary, middle, Interview 4)*

Achieving these successful outcomes confirmed to Neil that he had chosen the right actions, which, in turn, enhanced his self-efficacy and professional identity, as he and others demonstrated their 'capacity for self-reflection, self-regulation, and persistence ……self-efficacy, and moral responsibility to act' (Paris & Lung, 2008, p. 255).

Working with colleagues

Three teachers experienced contexts-for-action that involved their colleagues. Neil described how, prior to the pandemic, there had been little need for innovation. This meant fewer opportunities for mindful, intentional action and his job satisfaction waning. Paradoxically, the pandemic had given him 'another mountain to climb' (Interview 1), allowing him to implement a new whole-school approach to teaching his subject, and to rejuvenate his professional identity as a teacher who could act in ways that benefited pupils and colleagues. Similarly, Mia, was empowered to act when a colleague was absent during one of the lockdowns. This new context meant Mia becoming the only specialist teacher of her subject in her secondary school, and being given responsibility for planning and curriculum design, 'which I was really excited about, as it is an aspect of being a teacher I really enjoy and something that new teachers often don't have the opportunity to be involved with' (Journal 1). With the support of a colleague, Mia designed 'the new curriculum using her specialist knowledge and her teaching experience' (Journal 1), strengthening a professional identity associated with having strong subject knowledge. Like Neil, Mia's experience shows how teacher agency can be achieved through working successfully with colleagues.

In contrast, Gina spoke of complaints from colleagues about the timing of well-intentioned decisions which had negatively impacted on their wellbeing.

> I think there's a bit of a misunderstanding as well, with decisions and things that have been put into place have happened a bit quickly and felt a bit like we hadn't planned them out. And yet we're just constantly in this what still feels like a bit of a warzone battle, of having to make decisions very quickly and so a lot of our leadership has been much more direct; 'right, we've got to do this, get on with it. Here's the information, here's the instruction.' And that probably does feel like it's them and us, so we've had a culture that's developed this term that has felt a little bit more not where I want it to be.
>
> *(Gina, secondary, middle, Interview 4)*

By blaming contextual factors that were beyond her control, Gina was able to sustain her sense of professional identity. This was further strengthened by working collaboratively with a colleague to organise a development event for staff.

> Meeting this colleague has re-ignited my passion for planning and delivering high quality CPD [continuing professional development] next year. It also allowed me to reflect on the fact that I haven't really worked with anyone else who does the role that I do for many years now. It's so important to find people who can not only discuss ideas and their potential impact on the same level, as well as to find that peer-to-peer support that I spend so much time cultivating for other groups of staff I work with in my role.
>
> *(Gina, secondary, middle, Journal 3)*

Widely cited research (Lave & Wenger, 1991; Wenger, 1998) has shown that educational contexts which promote communities of practice (where social interaction and collegiality is encouraged), support teachers to develop their professional identity and stay committed to their work. It could be argued that these are also important contexts for teacher agency. Having the opportunity to design a CPD event, enabled Gina to reinforce what, to her, was an important part of her professional identity.

Emotional work

Like the teachers in Buchanan's (2015) study of teacher identity and agency, for Anna, Lucy, Neil and Mia, acting in ways that allowed them to utilise their capabilities for the benefit of pupils' learning outcomes (and, for Neil, Mia and Gina, to benefit colleagues too) strengthened their sense of self-efficacy and professional identities.

Emotional work

Professional identities are permeated, as much teaching is, by emotions. Emotions and their management are integral to teachers' work, as they navigate the complex worlds of classroom and staffroom, learning and teaching, and external expectations and demands. Teachers also invest themselves and their emotions in their work to care about and for their pupils (Day & Gu, 2010; Kelchtermans, 2009; Nias, 1997; O'Connor, 2008; see Chapter 7). Professional identities are, therefore, not just about how teachers feel about themselves, but also how they feel about their pupils (James-Wilson, 2001, cited in Day & Gu, 2010).

The pandemic emphasised the importance of all teachers' feelings towards their pupils, but it was predominantly the early-phase teachers who reflected on how the pandemic had shone a light on this emotional aspect of their work, leading them to adjust their professional identities. This was most significant for five out of the six early-phase secondary teachers, who had previously formed their identities around their subject and giving pupils the required knowledge for exam success.

For example, Patricia and Max admitted that they had initially been drawn into teaching due to a desire to teach their subject, but the pandemic had shifted how they saw their role towards a greater focus on their relationships with their pupils. As a pastoral head of year, Max was responsible for helping pupils and their families navigate the turmoil of the pandemic. He found that building empathic relationships with his pupils had become a key part of his professional identity.

> Sometimes I think people ... think 'Well I can come in, I've got this knowledge, you're going to sit down and listen.' – it doesn't work like that. You've got to be able to build relationships. You've got to be able to get on the students' wavelength. Be humble in yourself and try and empathise with where they're coming from... If I didn't have empathy with them, I'd be doing them a massive disservice.
>
> *(Max, secondary, early, Interview 4)*

Their ability to understand and share their pupils' feelings, in order to intervene appropriately, shaped how these teachers understood what it meant to be a teacher and, in turn, how they constructed their professional selves.

Other secondary teachers reflected on how the pandemic had changed how they felt towards their pupils. Anna felt galvanised to fight for more professional

Professional identities **77**

mental health support in schools, securing a professional identity based around advocating for pupils' needs.

> It's made me even more assured that I am an activist and will continue to be one within the education system. And I think that word is a word that I have been not sure about using about myself. But I feel quite strongly about that.
>
> *(Anna, primary, early, Interview 3)*

Anna recognised a role for herself in preparing pupils for a successful, happy life beyond school which, for her, went beyond ensuring they achieved good exam grades. She was concerned about the impact of the pandemic on her pupils' wellbeing, having noticed that many were struggling with their emotions. As such, Anna's professional identity became multifaceted.,

> part parent, part counsellor, part first-aider, part teacher, part friend, part disciplinarian. As an educator, as a teacher, you have all these facets to the job anyway. Now I'm also their Covid correspondent... that's been more complex because that is part scientist, part lateral flow expert and, also, part ... trauma responder.
>
> *(Anna, primary, early, Interview 3)*

> It's the safeguarding, it's the teaching, it's the extra curriculum, it's the liaising with parents, it's the nurture and pastoral roles that we play as tutors and just as teachers in general of young people. It's the most wonderful and intense, but completely all-encompassing thing. I don't think you can be a professional teacher without any one of those elements.
>
> *(Anna, primary, early, Interview 4)*

For Anna, her identity also involved having the courage and vulnerability to share her emotions with pupils.

> Being human with your children, I think, is a big one for me. Show them the vulnerability, show them the frustration, show them the sadness. I think especially throughout the pandemic, for me, when it was very, very close and we were worried... when they got sent home and I was sad with them. I think that's important because I think it teaches them how to deal with healthy emotion. I think that is courageous and ... we sometimes think that 'professionalism' has no heart... There's something about professionalism that means you have to be stoic. I disagree with that. Having a real sense of vulnerability is important to me.
>
> *(Anna, primary, early, Interview 4)*

78 Professional identities

Anna revealed the complexity of teachers' emotional work during the pandemic, which meant fulfilling many roles, being honest about her own vulnerabilities and, subsequently, reassessing and reforming her professional identity.

Unlike the secondary teachers, early-phase primary teachers did not note subject knowledge as part of their professional identity. However, three teachers did comment on the emotional aspects of their role. For example, Lucy revealed the depth of emotion that she felt for her pupils, investing a lot of time and emotional capital to ensure she had 'really solid' relationships and 'meaningful moments' with her pupils (Interview 5). And for Cate, despite questioning whether she would stay in the profession due to what she saw as a lack of support from senior leaders (see Chapter 2), witnessing detrimental effects of the pandemic on pupils' learning and behaviour strengthened a professional identity that was based on being emotionally invested in her pupils and building caring relationships with them.

> There's one child (let's call him Tom), who I have followed through school. He struggles with behaviour and academically. I have always had a lot of time for Tom. I know he wants, more than anything, to do well in life, but he has a lot of outside factors creating barriers for him. As well as having SEN needs and being from a low-income family, in recent years he's become a young carer. Throughout the last two years and the lockdowns, Tom was in a different class to mine, and his behaviour deteriorated. I have a fond memory of calling Tom's mum at the end of last year to inform her that he'd be back in my class again, she was so happy, there were tears. I was determined to ensure that Tom's final year at primary school was a successful one, knowing that I had done everything in my power to help him build a successful future at secondary!
>
> Tom has low self-esteem; he feels like the world is against him and finds it hard to trust others. He'll be quick to fight back with anger when he feels that he has been wronged, those without understanding of Tom can often mistake this for intentional rudeness. Tom needs to know that you believe in him, and I truly do, which is why I chose to have him in my group for our morning revision lessons. I knew it was going to be a challenge as Tom's academic levels were somewhat lower than the rest of the group and I was also conscious of his self-esteem, I didn't want it to have a negative effect. I had an open and honest chat with Tom and we both agreed that we wanted to see how it went. I couldn't be prouder, I saw Tom's self-esteem flourish in the groups, he was asking for extra work to take home and I could see his pride in the progress he'd made. Alongside this there was a change in Tom's behaviour, he wasn't disruptive in lessons, he sat quietly listening to my every word, he began to work more collaboratively with other children without arguments and his anger appeared less frequently.

> Sadly, due to personal circumstance, Tom never got to sit his SATs papers, which is a shame. He worked so hard to have a real chance of getting an 'age-related' score which could have been another great victory for his self-esteem. I hope that moving on, Tom has another teacher that believes in him, someone to champion even those small successes. One day he won't need that, he'll be his own cheerleader, but for now, he still needs a role model, someone that will continue to show him the way and help him realise his wonderful potential.
>
> *(Extract from Cate's journal)*

Cate's portrait of Tom reveals the extent of her emotional investment in her pupils. Caring for Tom involved making time to boost his self-esteem, communicate with him and his mother and consider his individual difficulties when interacting with him. Believing that her emotional investment was responsible for Tom's success boosted Cate's self-efficacy and secured a professional identity based on caring deeply for her pupils (also see Chapter 7).

Thus, understanding and managing their own and others' emotions are keys aspects of teachers' work, and their success or otherwise in doing so, is a significant contributor to their sense of professional identity (Day, 2018).

Making a difference: meeting the needs of disadvantaged pupils

> Knowing the difference you make to the children's lives. Knowing that no matter what anybody in government or whoever else, no matter what they're saying, I don't care. I know that we make a big difference for these children's lives, and they appreciate you every day. And that's why you do it.
>
> *(Teresa, primary, middle, Interview 4)*

As the chapters in this book continue to demonstrate, strong moral purpose and a belief that they can make a difference are key to many teachers' professional identities, enabling them to make sense of their work, navigate policy changes, stay motivated and teach to their best (Buchanan, 2015; Day & Gu, 2010). For primary and secondary teachers across the career phases in six of the ten schools, the pandemic revealed clear inequalities and inequities within their local school communities. As Dawn stated,

> I realise more than ever now that for some of our children, the only way out of their difficult situations is through education.
>
> *(Dawn, primary, later, Journal 3)*

For Max, who worked in a school that was in the same deprived area where he had grown up, the pandemic caused him to reflect that, without having succeeded within the education system, he could have been in the same

80 Professional identities

position as some of his pupils' families who were really struggling. Consequently, being passionate about wanting to make a difference to his pupils, so they could escape poverty, became a stronger part of his professional identity. Emma's professional identity was also bound up in her feelings towards pupils from disadvantaged backgrounds. The pandemic cemented her commitment to caring for them and making a difference to their lives.

> I like knowing that I'm doing a good job for the kids who really need it. They tug on my heartstrings. I'm the kind of teacher that opens my heart, not in it for the money, and I really care. I've had children coming to school with no breakfast, no clean clothes and I do whatever I can to overcome it. We have lots of children from split families, and I'm the only stable thing in their lives.
>
> *(Emma, primary, middle, Interview 1)*

Empathy for pupils' individual contexts, wellbeing, and personal difficulties became a greater part of Gina's professional identity. Gina recognised that successful outcomes for some pupils could be feeling safe and valued in school and being part of a community, rather than just gaining academic qualifications. And Neil (who worked in the same school as Gina) had come to realise that previously important aspects of his professional identity, such as looking smart and being punctual, were insignificant compared to supporting pupils' personal and social development.

Rose's identity was rooted in care, not just for her pupils but also their families, which motivated her to act to address the immediate inequalities she saw within her school community. Inspired by Marcus Rashford (a famous footballer who coordinated getting food to poorer families during the pandemic), Rose helped to set up a foodbank in her school for parents who had been furloughed or made redundant. As well as providing essential support to her school community, the foodbank gave her greater insight into her pupils' home circumstances. As a result, Rose constructed a professional identity based on being a teacher who supported every pupil to have higher aspirations and skills for a successful life.

> You've got to be seen to be fair to everybody, to give everybody the best possible opportunities, but also, you've got to do what you think is right for the best of each of the kids, and every child is different – the way you deal with one child might be completely different to the way you deal with another child.
>
> *(Rose, secondary, later, Interview 4)*

Jane, who worked in a school where she described many pupils coming from families with a history of unemployment, found the pandemic had shifted her professional identity towards a greater focus on supporting pupils' holistic development. COVID-19 restrictions had meant having to organise her school differently and Jane witnessing pupils thriving when able to be more creative and active. Jane also reflected that some pupils could not see the point of some of the academic learning they had to do, especially if they found it difficult. She therefore reconstructed her professional identity to accommodate a focus on broadening her pupils' horizons, showing them paths that were not just based on academic attainment, and giving them transferable skills (such as problem-solving) and life skills (such as how to present yourself). However, she was also concerned that this would not be possible if educational systems and priorities returned to how they were pre-pandemic.

> For me personally, [the pandemic] has made me question what our education system is really about and how effective it is for many children. Surely there should be more emphasis on developing secure, happy, independent, well-rounded individuals who can communicate and work constructively with others? I still love working with the children but I'm not sure what we are doing for them is the right thing – but I don't know the answer. I have found myself asking more questions but feel that many will never be answered, and some even totally forgotten about as day-to-day life resumes.
>
> *(Jane, primary, later, Journal 3)*

For teachers in all phases of their career, it seemed the pandemic forced them to reflect on their work, its purposes, and their pupils' needs, prompting them to renegotiate what it meant to them 'to make a difference' and, in turn, their professional identities.

Conclusion

Teachers' professional identities evolve and fluctuate over time, in response to different experiences and contexts. The pandemic changed teachers' work, creating powerful emotions such as self-doubt and vulnerability, but which in some cases also enabled opportunities for learning and acting courageously, strengthening some teachers' sense of self-efficacy, and reshaping beliefs about themselves as professionals and their understanding of what it meant to do their best for the pupils in their care (see Figure 6.1).

Where teachers chose to act in ways that had a positive impact on pupils' learning outcomes, their self-efficacy and professional identities were strengthened, but where their actions were restricted, they were more likely to doubt their abilities, and their self-efficacy and professional identities were threatened. At the same time, the pandemic highlighted the emotional nature of teachers' work as teachers witnessed pupils struggling with their mental wellbeing and behaviour. These experiences led many teachers to view their commitment to building positive relationships with their pupils as a key part

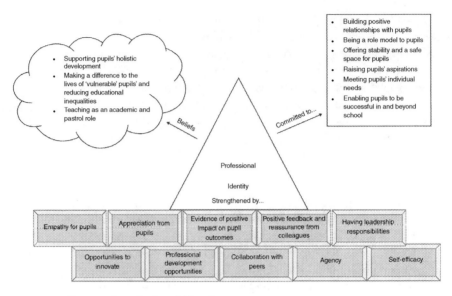

FIGURE 6.1 Facets of professional identity

of their professional identity. Furthermore, for teachers working in schools serving poorer communities, the pandemic, and the new ways of working it necessitated, shifted the way they thought about how they could 'make a difference'. Underpinned by empathy, they saw themselves as teachers who believed in supporting pupils' holistic development and could offer a range of opportunities and experiences so pupils could go on to have successful, happy lives beyond school. In this way, the pandemic led to many teachers' reconstructing their professional identities, and consequently a stronger sense of moral purpose, motivation and commitment to their work.

7

COMMITMENT TO CARE

> You certainly have to care. You have to care.
>
> *(Cate, primary, early, Interview 4)*

Introduction

This chapter examines how teachers from all career phases cared for their pupils as they navigated their way through the pandemic. The chapter begins by examining how different ways of working offered an opportunity for teachers to develop greater empathy for pupils' and families' circumstances, resulting in them caring in new and unexpected ways. It then explores how teachers cared for their pupils' social and emotional wellbeing, prioritising this over and above academic learning and, at times, caring for themselves. Finally, the chapter moves to consider the emotional and professional costs for two teachers who had to prioritise care for themselves.

Research into teacher-pupil relationships has repeatedly shown that caring is seen by many teachers as a key part of their role (e.g., Acker, 1995; Barber, 2002; Nias, 1989). In her exploration of caring, Noddings (2013) defined 'caring about' as concern for another but not responding to that feeling, and 'caring for' as part of a caring relationship, requiring personal contact, attention and response. For teachers then, caring *about* their pupils is not enough. They must also care *for* pupils through building relationships with them, paying attention to them and responding to their needs. But, to properly understand their pupils' needs so they can respond appropriately, teachers also require empathy. Empathy is therefore a key component of caring (Noddings, 2013).

Many researchers have examined teacher empathy (see, for example, Bullough, 2019a, 2019b; Cooper, 2004; Meyers et al., 2019; Swan & Riley, 2015) showing it to be a complex concept with multiple meanings in different

DOI: 10.4324/9781003391661-7

84 Commitment to care

contexts. It is 'an important skill, as it represents the very foundations for student care' (Swan & Riley, 2015, p. 228)

However, taken together, we can deduce that empathic teachers are those who make an effort to listen and pay careful attention to their pupils, 'feel with' them and are moved to make a caring response (Bullough, 2019b; Noddings, 2013). Yet care is complex and requires considerable empathy (Day, 2004, p. 28).

Caring *about* pupils (how teachers feel about them) and caring *for* pupils (empathic teachers taking deliberate, purposeful action) also makes teaching an emotional practice (Gay, 2018), where what teachers do and how they do it reveals them 'as highly moral individuals who attach themselves mentally and emotionally to their students and generate similar responses in return' (Cooper, 2004, p. 12).

As earlier chapters have shown, primary and secondary teachers from each career phase talked about the considerable amount of emotional work they carried out in caring for pupils who had to contend with a range of personal and academic challenges. As a result of this caring work, these teachers built strong emotional attachments to their pupils and reshaped their professional identities.

Developing empathy for pupils and their families

At the start of the study, Orla described feeling more emotionally connected and empathic towards her pupils.

> It's been a really tough year for students, and I really feel for them. You feel more closely connected than you did prior to the pandemic, emotionally as well as in other ways.
>
> *(Orla, secondary, middle, Interview 1)*

As a result of feeling for her pupils, Orla became more focused on her relationships with them, changing her usual practice to allow for more time to getting to know them as individuals.

> I've focussed more than ever on my relationships with the students, because many haven't been in school for a number of months, and I am wanting to make their classroom experience as positive as I can, taking a personal interest in them, finding out more about them as people... being a role model, showing respect, establishing respectful relationships.
>
> *(Orla, secondary, middle, Interview 1)*

When considering what 'good' teaching looked like during the pandemic, Max (secondary, early) emphasised empathy as a key attribute. He empathised with pupils and families who he saw struggling to navigate their way through

Commitment to care **85**

this turbulent time and tried to offer them reassurance. Similarly, Alan (primary, middle) who was given responsibility for communicating with 'vulnerable pupils' families during the second lockdown, found himself developing greater empathy for those that were struggling. 'You get to see a different side of how families cope... how some families were getting on okay while others were struggling. So, I feel, I felt for them' (Interview 1). Teresa and Cate developed empathy for parents who were trying to support multiple children at home. Teresa cared for these families by offering for their children to return to school with the 'vulnerable' and keyworkers' children, whilst Cate cared for her pupils' anxious mothers by listening to them.

> It was harder for parents ... There were so many children at home that there just wasn't enough adult support. So, we were able to offer places to people and that felt good. That felt really good ... With parents that were struggling we've given them the place that they needed in school.
> *(Teresa, primary, middle, Interview 2)*

> Some of my phone-calls were tough, I had some mothers that were suffering high anxiety themselves due to the pandemic. I listened. I don't think people realise that as a teacher you are sometimes a support for parents too and how important that is; not everybody is fortunate enough to have good friends to lean on.
> *(Cate, primary, early, Journal 1)*

When schools fully reopened after the first lockdown, Fern's empathy and care for her pupils were reflected in her standing at the school gate every morning to check on their physical and emotional wellbeing. She believed she would notice if there was something wrong with a pupil and could then do something to support them. Like Fern at the school gates, Michelle commented that at the start of each lesson she was now trying to empathise with her pupils' emotional state so she could offer the care they needed: 'The routine and the habit of teaching [has changed, you] almost have to check in with your class on that empathetic level every day just to take the temperature of the room' (Michelle, primary, later, Interview 4).

Fern hoped that her colleagues, who had been making welfare phone calls to families during the lockdowns, had developed greater empathy for their pupils and families and, in turn, a greater understanding of how they can make a difference to pupils' lives.

> Staff were making welfare calls which they would never have done before just to check people were alright... I'm hoping they've become a bit more empathetic to some of the situations that some of the families may have been in. And also, maybe a bit more understanding about some of

86 Commitment to care

the challenges of children... So maybe there's a greater understanding of what's required of them as teachers whilst the children are in school and how important it is.

(Fern, primary, later, Interview 4)

For Gina, developing greater empathy for pupils and their families had made her think about how she could care for pupils simply by talking with them, giving them a sense of belonging and making them feel safe and valued.

If I'm thinking about it now, I would say that there's so much more weight that has to be given to a much broader context of children and all of their own personal difficulties and emotional issues and well-being and mental state... I don't think it's changed it so far that I now feel differently about wanting good outcomes for kids, in terms of things like qualifications and so on. It's not touched that aspect of it. But a good outcome for some kids is just about having a conversation with them and making them feel valued and sort of part of a school and a community and really being quite a safe place for them compared sometimes to home.

(Gina, secondary, middle, Interview 4)

Gina now included empathy as an attribute of 'good' teachers, linking it with listening to pupils, trying to understand them and showing that they want to help.

Listening, and empathy, and understanding, and humour, and all those things - they're all about relationships, aren't they?... a good teacher will always seek to listen and understand, and to know their pupils and to show them that they want to be there and help them, because funnily enough, not all teachers do that.

(Gina, secondary, middle, Interview 4)

Teachers serving the poorest communities across England cared for families suffering hardship, through distributing food parcels and vouchers, and even setting up their own food banks (Moss et al., 2020). Rose's empathy and care for pupils and their families extended to setting up a foodbank in her school after realising there were problems with the government's food voucher scheme at the same time as parents were losing their jobs. Rose gave up a considerable of her own time to organise the distribution of food parcels to vulnerable families.

Just the realisation when you get an email from the parent who said, 'I've seen the thing about the foodbank, is there any possibility that you can help me because I'm a single parent, and I'm self-employed? I've got my children at home; I can't go to work so I've got no income coming in.'

(Rose, secondary, later, Interview 1).

Through setting up the foodbank, Rose had greater contact with parents than usual, learned more about pupils' home circumstances and developed even greater empathy for what families were going through. This gave her a sense of purpose and determination to keep caring for the pupils and families that needed her help.

> You think you know the kids but actually how much do you actually know about them? There's a boy at the school who asked for help from the foodbank because his mum and sisters were out at work and, at 13, he was in charge of the house. Some are struggling due to no fault of their own.
>
> *(Rose, secondary, later, Interview 2)*

Building trusting relationships with families, empathising with them and knowing she was caring for them helped Teresa to feel positive about her work.

> As a school... we've been really conscious of the children that need help, the children that need support. And we've put that support in place for them. And I think because of that, we've come to know our families a lot more than we used to. And our families have come to trust us a lot more than they used to. So, I think there's definitely some positives that have come out of it.
>
> *(Teresa, primary, middle, Interview 4)*

In this way, the different ways of working during the pandemic highlighted the difficulties that many families were experiencing, leading some teachers to 'feel with' their pupils and families, pay close attention to them and respond by caring for them in different ways. The next section focuses on teachers whose empathy led them to care for their pupils' social and emotional wellbeing.

Putting pupils' social and emotional wellbeing first

> I think about them [the pupils] before I think about myself most of the time.
> *(Lucy, primary, early, Interview 3)*

From early March 2020, the start of the first lockdown, most people in England were confined to their homes. This meant children only seeing other members of their household, with many poorer children also having to endure cramped conditions without access outside space, putting considerable strain on their social and emotional wellbeing. From 1 June 2020, pupils in Reception (ages four to five), Year 1 (ages five to six) and Year 6 (ages ten to eleven) were prioritised for returning to school, but other year groups took longer to return and often only consisted of the pupils deemed 'vulnerable' or with keyworker parents. And, although schools in England reopened to all in

88 Commitment to care

September 2020, ongoing COVID-19 outbreaks meant classes, 'bubbles' (groups of classes that only mixed with each other) and even whole schools having to close at short notice.

Blanden et al. (2021), who analysed the impact of the first lockdown on five- to eleven-year olds' emotional and behavioural wellbeing using the 'Strengths and Difficulties Questionnaire in the UK Household Longitudinal Study', found an increase in difficulties for pupils who spent the most time away from school. Similarly, Cowie and Myers (2021) drawing on the results of various international research, showed that the closure of schools, which meant reduced contact with friends and increased exposure to media coverage of the pandemic, negatively affected young people's social and emotional wellbeing. As already illustrated, teachers who made weekly phone calls to their pupils and their families during this time developed a greater understanding of their pupils' home lives. This was the same for primary teachers across England who empathised with pupils living in overcrowded, poor households and struggling to engage with home learning, and cared for them by prioritising their social and emotional needs over academic learning when they returned to school after the first lockdown (Moss et al, 2020).

But a third lockdown (January to March 2021) meant schools again only being open to pupils who were considered 'vulnerable' or whose parents were keyworkers, and many pupils' wellbeing continuing to suffer. This extended time away from school revealed to pupils, teachers and parents that schools offered more than academic learning. Schools also provided socialisation, structure and purpose, which pupils needed for their social and emotional wellbeing (Buchanan et al., 2022). Blanden et al. (2021) and Buchanan et al. (2022) therefore concluded that, given the 'strong links between students' mental health and their educational progress and achievement' (Blanden et al, 2021, p. 4), schools would need to support pupil's recovery by continuing to focus on caring for pupils' social and emotional wellbeing.

Without caring for pupils' wellbeing, 15 primary and secondary teachers (representing each career phase) realised that pupils were unlikely to be able to engage in academic learning. Fern stated that the pandemic had given her 'permission that actually caring for the children and their families and trying to backfill all that social stuff is actually important, because otherwise if you don't backfill that, you can't move them forward academically' (Interview 1). Fern became increasingly concerned about pupils' mental health and wellbeing as she witnessed some banging their heads against the wall. Yet, with little support available from social care services, school staff, including herself, were having to act as social workers and therapists e.g., supervising parent/child visits, providing evidence for social work case reports with no notice, and providing counselling in school.

> They were asking so much more of us, and they were a long time before they went back to face to face. Some speech therapists, some counselling services, are wanting to do it online. No, you actually need that human

warmth and interaction ... We go to the ends of the earth for the children, and we try and bend over backwards ... But actually, our main term of reference is to teach the children and give them knowledge ... I can't do it without making sure they're fed, making sure that they feel safe, making sure they're happy, and making sure we try and make their time whilst they're here as joyful as possible.

(Fern, primary, later, Interview 4)

Similarly, Teresa (primary, middle) recognised that teachers needed to care for pupils' wellbeing before they could focus on academic learning. She asserted, 'I don't think learning is the first thing we need to worry about. I think the first thing we need to worry about is their wellbeing. We need to make sure they're OK. We can't underestimate the personal impact.' (Interview 2) and later, 'I think the emphasis on mental health and children's mental health has been strengthened. So, I think, as a school, I think that has to be our new purpose.' (Interview 5).

Other teachers noticed pupils struggling with their wellbeing when they returned to schools after the third lockdown. 'There was definitely a difference in the behaviours of students coming back, and their coping mechanisms, and where they were mentally' (Neil, secondary, middle, Interview 2). Neil felt that whilst the first lockdown had felt more like an extended holiday, the third one meant pupils 'dealing with remote learning for such an extended period of time, doing everything on screens, and so they noticeably came back a little bit diminished' (Interview 2). He observed children who were withdrawn, and others panicking about being behind in their learning. Some had also suffered from not being able to spend time with friends and engage in extra-curricular activities. 'It's had a real tangible impact on their wellbeing and who they are as children, and that makes them vulnerable' (Interview 2). Additionally, Neil was concerned about pupils with special educational needs and disabilities (SEND) who had struggled the most with remote learning and were struggling to reintegrate back into school. Thus, he also believed that there needed to be a greater focus on supporting pupils' mental health and social development, rather than on academic attainment.

Emma and Kath worried about the impact of the pandemic on the wellbeing of pupils in their schools too, recognising that teachers would need to care for those who were suffering due to family hardship, spotting signs of distress quickly so support could be put in place.

Because of the demographic of the area that the school is, then we're going to see families affected by lockdown, furlough, or even losing jobs. But I think as teachers we're going to have to keep a closer eye on our children just to try and identify things before they get too serious... I think maybe that kind of social care aspect of the teacher's role is going to be a bit more over the coming months.

(Emma, primary, middle, Interview 2)

90 Commitment to care

Gina was also concerned about pupils' wellbeing and started to implement measures to support them. During the first lockdown, as part of her responsibilities, Gina had restructured tutor groups so that each group had only one tutor, whereas previously they may have had two or three. She felt that this change had strengthened the form tutor role as it enabled teachers to build caring, empathic relationship with their pupils' through sharing their experiences of the pandemic. 'Everybody's felt quite responsible for their tutor groups and their wellbeing, and that has become much, much stronger, I would say' (Interview 2). In an online tutor session focused on wellbeing, Gina found that,

> a lot of students really opened up, even though they're online, really opened up about experiences and things that they'd gone through, and a lot of the tutors said to us it was a really valuable session… it did get a lot of good feedback and I think they needed that opportunity to just share what some of them had gone through or experienced or were experiencing.
>
> *(Gina, secondary, middle, Interview 2)*

Anna cared about her pupils' social and emotional wellbeing. Although everyone was having to adjust to living in a pandemic, she recognised this was the not the same for everyone. For example, some pupils missed being able to take part in sport whilst others missed family members who had died after contracting COVID-19. Anna felt that the impact of the pandemic on pupils' wellbeing could be long-lasting.

> We are not fully seeing the results of this yet. It's too soon. We can't really process the trauma whilst we are in the trauma, and we are all still living it. There's only so much that I think the kids are showing. It's coming out in little bursts, in little moments, conversations that they have. They are processing it. I think it's going to affect us for a long time.
>
> *(Anna, secondary, early, Interview 1)*

In her role as a form tutor, Anna showed empathy and care for her pupils. For example, she tried to reassure them when their 'bubble' had to close due to someone testing positive for Covid and gave them a safe space to share how they were feeling.

> I tried to rally the troops as it were and say that they were part of a system that was saving people's lives and 'you going home and you making this sacrifice is about saving someone else's life and that's amazing'. And they're all distraught, looking at me and I said 'it's ok to feel angry, it's ok to feel sad, it's ok to feel, how do you feel? how do you feel? how do you feel?' and they were all like 'yes I feel really sad', 'I'm really angry', 'I feel

really disappointed'. One of the kids in my class turned around and said 'I'm actually really proud of us.' So, my job has got more complex because that's a whole new level of emotional work that we have had to do.

(Anna, secondary, early, Interview 2)

The way Anna talked about her pupils showed how caring for her pupils was an emotional practice which involved sharing emotional experiences (Hargreaves, 2001). This emotional work, whilst difficult, was also rewarding for Anna. She felt proud of the attachments she had made to her pupils and the courage they had shown in continuing to engage with school despite struggling with their wellbeing.

I've just bonded with them in such a phenomenal way, and I could get emotional talking about it.

(Anna, secondary, early, Interview 2)

Courage for me is standing in the face of something frightening ... kids themselves have faced massive uncertainty. They have faced massive unknowns. They have faced literal illness, literal death, literal bereavement. And they've come to school and had a go. That's courage. That's courage. Massive amounts ... We need to take a good hard look at what these kids have gone through, what we have gone through, and start recognising that this is a trauma. It is a social trauma that has affected our social lives.

(Anna, secondary, early, Interview 3)

It was important to Anna that this trauma was recognised more widely so that pupils could get the right sort of care to ensure their recovery. Her commitment to caring her pupils' wellbeing therefore extended beyond her own classroom to appealing for government funding so schools could employ mental health professionals.

It will be the thing that I will bang on about until the end of my time as a teacher, because... I just don't understand... why every school doesn't have a budget that is set aside specifically to hire a full time, fully qualified mental health professional.

(Anna, secondary, early, Interview 3)

The costs of personal vulnerability

As well as investing their emotions in caring for pupils, three teachers often put pupils' needs before their own, showing how a commitment to care also

92 Commitment to care

challenges teachers' ability to manage their work and personal lives. Kath (secondary, early) felt she had shown courage by going into school whilst waiting to be vaccinated (the UK government did not prioritise teachers for vaccines like they did for other keyworkers). But she put the children's wellbeing first because 'the kids are coming to school, no one else is going to teach them. We've got to be there for them' (Interview 3). Similarly, Cate's (primary, early) commitment to caring for her pupils meant that 'throughout the pandemic, I put myself and my family at risk every day by just showing up and I do that because of my commitment to the children in my care' (Journal 2). Cate described herself as 'genuinely invested in these lovely children that I teach, and I do care about them' (Interview 2).

Lucy (primary, early) also put her pupils' wellbeing before her own and her family's. She was scared that she would catch COVID-19 at school and pass it on. 'Every time I come into work that's what I think about on the way to work. I think about it when the children are in the classroom. I think about it every day' (Interview 1). Although this worry impacted on Lucy's emotional wellbeing, which she described as feeling a huge sense of responsibility, being 'at risk', and 'on the edge all the time' (Interview 1), she felt the leadership team at her school had done the right thing in prioritising care for pupils. 'Throughout the whole thing, all of the choices were made for the children, and I think that's all you can ask for from school is that they put their children first' (Interview 1).

In contrast, two middle-phase teachers, Emma (primary) and Mark (secondary), were not able to put their pupils' needs first due to their own clinically vulnerable status. But through prioritising their personal lives over their work lives, they found themselves estranged from colleagues, whom they felt did not empathise or care for them, and their mental health suffered.

Despite having documentation which stated she was clinically vulnerable, Emma found that 'management were very reluctant to accept that I needed to be shielded' and she felt 'very unsupported by the school' (Interview 1). When she did return to school, she

> had no contact from SLT (senior leadership team) until two days before I came back, telling me that there was no PPE (personal protective equipment) for me for the next two weeks. So, I've come back, but now there is no preparation time. It just feels like I am being punished. It's frowned on to be off sick.
>
> *(Emma, primary, middle, Interview 1)*

Emma ate her lunch on her own so she could avoid the 'crowded' staffroom and did not mix with anyone outside school. She felt that leaders were dismissive of her concerns about catching COVID-19 from another teacher or child, expecting her to attend in-person staff meetings.

Commitment to care **93**

> Yesterday's staff meeting was face to face, and I was in a room with ten other staff, eight of which I don't normally meet… this is not protecting me, but I can't refuse to go. All I can do is to sit in a corner with my mask on. I find it difficult to cope. I am genuinely worried that if I catch the virus, it's life or death. Then your husband says to you, 'I don't want you to go to school because I don't want you to catch this virus, I don't want to lose you yet'.
>
> *(Emma, primary, middle, Interview 1)*

When Emma voiced concerns about being in school due to her vulnerability, her head teacher told her that if she followed the safety protocols they had put in place, she would be safer in school than in a supermarket.

> On my return to school in September, I was extremely nervous and felt 'out of the loop' I had to rebuild my relationships with colleagues and children and during my absence felt that my role within the school had changed dramatically. I felt that my shielding was an inconvenience to the school and that they didn't believe that I should have shielded despite the letters I had received from the government. I was very upset when my subject coordinator role, which I had held successfully for six years, was given to another member of staff and I was given an additional subject to oversee two days before the end of the school year, having done most of the my own subject preparation work for this academic year. I was worried about going into the staffroom as there was no way of socially distancing at lunchtime. In addition, there was no sanitising equipment to use on photocopiers and cutters. I did request this, but they just put a cloth and some spray into the staffroom that no one else bothered to use. I had taken to sitting in the lower hall by myself to each my lunch each day and this increased my feelings of isolation and loneliness. It was about this time that I began to question whether I wanted to remain being a teacher (for the first time ever).
>
> *(Emma, primary, middle, Journal 1)*

After another period of shielding, Emma became worried about how her return to school would be received by her colleagues.

> I feel a bit undervalued by school as well - the senior leadership attitude to the fact that they don't think I should be shielding anyway. And I think because they've voiced that in open areas I kind of feel that that has permeated a little bit across the school.
>
> *(Emma, primary, middle, Interview 2)*

Emma no longer felt like a valued member of staff. Messages were not always passed on and decisions were made without her input. This led her to reassess her commitment to teaching.

94 Commitment to care

Because of what's happened, it's made me view things quite differently. You realise there is a life outside of school. I do have my family. I do have my husband and my dog, my kids. And some days I just don't want to touch schoolwork. I want to be able to have a weekend where I don't have to touch it.

(Emma, primary, middle, Interview 3)

Mark found working from home challenging. He felt that communication from the school was poor. Many conversations were not shared with him. He received a lot of emails but felt an occasional phone call or conversation on screen would have made him feel part of the team.

If I was, again, in a leadership role I would have serious concerns that staff don't feel supported or they're getting to the point where they're working to try and achieve the goals that the school's laid out but it's causing actual physical pain.

(Mark, secondary, middle, Interview 2)

Mark found himself physically and mentally struggling with spending up to 15 hours a day working on a computer delivering remote lessons and creating new lessons from scratch. He had spoken to senior leadership but did not feel they understood how hard it was for him, and how his disabilities made it worse.

When I finished crying… quite literally with frustration at the response, I said to them, really honestly, I said 'you know it's quite upsetting if you don't take into consideration what I'm telling you and what the reality of it is for me'.

(Mark, secondary, middle, Interview 2)

Mark contacted Human Resources, who asked him what would help. He suggested reducing his teaching timetable so that he had more time to plan. However, nothing was done. Consequently, Mark decided to put himself first, by taking a day off and then deciding to reduce the content he was expected to teach. And when he returned to school the following term, he resolved not to take any work home and to say 'no' to extra responsibilities or tasks.

Whilst Mark and Emma's experiences diminished their resilience, caring for others bolstered Teresa's sense of pride and resilience.

It's made me realise what you are capable of doing… that I never realised as a school we have to do, sorting out breakfast parcels, counselling parents and trying to work out which children had a place in school and which children didn't have a place in school, and how we could help the children that were at home to carry on learning. All those things. The things that you never trained for as a teacher. And so yeah, the things that we've had to learn how to do, has definitely increased resilience and made us, made me, realise we can do it. And that maybe there is more to school than just teaching... what an important place school is for, not just for the children, but for the families that we serve as well. Because we're the people they came to when they were struggling. They called us. You know how we're trying to work out how we can help somebody because they've got no food. That's not traditionally what our role was. So yeah, definitely more resilient.

(Teresa, primary, middle, Interview 5)

Conclusion

As primary and secondary teachers cared for pupils and their families, the pandemic highlighted that 'schooling is about much more than learning' (Moss, 2020, p. 4). Weekly phone calls to families to check on pupils' wellbeing, the opening of schools to 'vulnerable' and keyworkers' children, and the provision of food parcels, meant teachers learning more about their pupils' individual circumstances. Consequently, many teachers developed greater empathy for them and their families, which led to a commitment to not just care *about* them, but care *for* them through paying attention to them, sharing experiences, listening, seeking to understand, and valuing them. Previous research, such as Barber's (2002) ethnographic study in an Australian high school serving a 'disadvantaged' community, has shown that teachers often express care for pupils when they believe their parents to be unsupportive, neglectful, welfare-dependent, and not valuing education. As a result, teachers care for their pupils in ways they believe are lacking in their homes, and their belief that pupils depend on their care sustains their commitment to teaching. Yet, during the pandemic, it seems some teachers were more likely to reject this deficit view of parents, demonstrating a greater understanding of why families were struggling and a strong motivation to do what they could to help them.

As all pupils returned to schools after lockdowns, many teachers were particularly worried about the impact of the pandemic on pupils' social and emotional wellbeing, realising that many pupils were also struggling with their mental health due to missing the socialisation, structure and purpose that schools offered. Teachers felt that support for pupils' wellbeing needed to be prioritised. Without this, pupils were unlikely to be able to engage effectively with academic learning or pass exams. For some teachers, this meant trying to be social workers and therapists, caring for pupils who they noticed were self-harming, anxious, withdrawn, bereaved, or distressed.

But there were two teachers who were not involved in this caring work as they were deemed to be 'clinically vulnerable' and had to prioritise caring for themselves. This meant being isolated from pupils and colleagues, and feeling undervalued and uncared for, which negatively impacted their wellbeing and

96 Commitment to care

commitment to their work. However, caring is emotional work, and their colleagues were prioritising their work lives, putting their pupils' needs before their own, risking their own and their families' physical and mental health to care for pupils, which may account for why they were unable to also care for their absent colleagues. It took considerable emotional energy, resilience and courage to persevere with caring for their pupils during this turbulent time.

> For much of the time, teachers work in situations that may reasonably be described as difficult, personal, emotional and cognitively challenging, sometimes turbulent and occasionally violently disruptive. It requires courage to maintain a commitment over time, courage to persist in caring for every student in the class.
>
> *(Day, 2004, p. 30)*

Although the emotional costs of caring for pupils were high, the many teachers in the study who cared for them and their families were rewarded by the strong relationships they built with their pupils, developed greater empathy for them (which they came to view as a key attribute of 'good' teachers), and, in turn, were able to stay committed to doing their best for them.

8

ORGANISATIONAL BELONGING AND COMMITMENT

The importance of trust

Introduction

This chapter focuses on teachers' sense of: 'identification with the values and goals of the organization, willingness to exert effort on behalf of the organization, and commitment to stay in the organization.' (Mowday et al, 1982 cited in Ross and Gray, 2006, p. 181). All 36 teachers interviewed had experienced unprecedented challenges to the norms of teaching and learning during the pandemic. However, levels of individuals' commitment benefited from the effects of workplace environments. Together with teachers' internal sense of vocation, these had enabled most (31) to learn to manage successfully the continuing disruptions, discontinuities, changing role requirements, and increased workload that resulted from the pandemic. Research has consistently found that teacher wellbeing, and levels of commitment are associated with the working conditions, collegiality and trust, and the quality of leadership within schools (Chan et al., 2008; Ross & Gray, 2006; Klassen, 2010; Blömeke et al., 2017; Grillo & Kier, 2021; Liu et al., 2021). The few whose commitment had wavered (5) worked in schools in which their relationships with leaders and/ or colleagues had become dysfunctional. Their interviews and journals illustrated the important role that schools, as caring, trustful organisations, played in supporting teachers' capacities to manage and engage in processes of recovery from adversity; and complements earlier chapters which have focused on care, wellbeing and resilience. The chapter is divided into three parts: i) leadership quality and care; ii) cultures of trust; and iii) collegiality and belonging.

Leadership quality and care

Teachers rely primarily for their on-going commitment on two sources.

DOI: 10.4324/9781003391661-8

The first source is their inner sense of moral purpose, professional, professional identity, motivation, commitment and resilience. The second source that provides professional nourishment is the quality of the workplace environment. It is the school principal who has major responsibility for this.

(Day, 2017, p. 133)

Recent research about successful school leaders' work during the pandemic indicates the importance of the school in nurturing and sustaining a sense of belonging, claimed to be 'particularly important in increasing teachers' organisational commitment and reducing their emotional exhaustion and work disengagement' (Bjork et al., 2019, p. 957) as leaders helped to bring school communities together and enabled teachers to survive and thrive despite the many challenges they faced.

Head teachers and their leadership teams have always had the responsibility of assisting teachers to navigate, for example, negative external policy requirements (Shaked & Schechter, 2017; Hulme et al., 2021). Especially in the early phases of the pandemic, the ways they enacted these responsibilities took on a special significance as they and their teachers responded to the unpredictable, almost weekly, barrage of demands from government.

The speed and pace of change is one of the biggest challenges. Just having to change all the timetables in the break times, and there's so much information to absorb and getting use to new routines and practices... trying to squeeze everything in and trying to be consistent.... endless really.

(Gina, secondary, middle, Interview 1)

Teachers spoke of being appreciated by their leaders.

The positives were always getting thanked, and the headteacher would say, 'I know that the government aren't thanking teachers, but we want to thank you because we know you worked really hard and you're still here', and so we did get a lot of praise. So that was a positive and it was a lot of team morale.

(Margaret, primary, middle, Interview 4)

Listening to teachers

It was important to teachers that they knew why decisions were being made, that they could approach their leaders and that they would be listened to and understood.

That's one thing the school has been very good with at a leadership level, really listening to teachers, and it's not like a one size fits all because, in the past, if someone had said 'I'm really tired and struggling and need a couple of days off', it would have been like 'what are you talking about? Get on with it, that's ridiculous, it's your job.' Whereas just a couple of weeks ago one of my team requested to me 'I'm absolutely at my wits end, I cannot do this, I need a couple of days off' and I said 'I fully support it, I'll take it to the head teacher' and she supported it and said member of staff had two days off and didn't resolve all the problems but came back feeling a lot better. And I think that's the kind of human consideration that perhaps is more evident in leadership now than it would have been prior to the pandemic.

(Neil, secondary, middle, Interview 3)

This process of what Bryk and Schneider (2002 p.23) termed 'genuine listening' clearly enhanced teachers' self-esteem and strengthened their affiliation with colleagues and the school.

A decision to permit teachers to work from home for their planning, preparation and assessment time (PPA) at Greenfields Secondary was praised by Neil, for its practical benefits. This underlying trust in teachers served to simultaneously strengthen the bonds between teachers and leaders.

We've been given a lot more trust back now. Working from home and treating teachers as professionals who won't just 'bunk off' when it suits them. No one is in teaching for an easy ride. Now it's transformed. Teachers are encouraged to work from home when they are not teaching. They can build their work around their personal life needs. Collectively it adds to a much more healthy collective work-life balance.

(Neil, secondary, middle, Interview 1)

At Skyward Primary, communication links were established throughout the pandemic to ensure that each teaching team contained a member of the Senior Leadership Team (SLT) responsible for checks on their wellbeing. The close and continuing 'presence' of the headteacher and leaders was also important.

The head teacher, throughout the pandemic where we were working from home, made weekly phone calls to all her staff members to check on you. That obviously stopped once we were back in school, but that made the difference. There was no assumption that we were fine. And when she rang, she was genuinely ringing to ask how we were, not had we completed a piece of work. So, I think that's really one significant support that was there. She has continued that thread in terms of she will message on 'Messenger' or 'WhatsApp' towards the end of the week and say, 'Thank you for the week', 'Thank you for this term' and she always finishes her work emails with phrases like, 'As always, if there's anything I can do to

100 Organisational belonging and commitment

help.' and that's that. It was there prior to the pandemic, but is there much more now, so the tone of a number of senior leaders' emails has changed, their signing off tone, and they might not think it matters, but it does because the more you hear that people can be there for you, the easier you find it to go to them if you need to. So I would say that's been a real support.

(Michelle, primary, later, Interview 5)

This went beyond expressed intentions and reassurances, providing evidence of 'the capacity of the school principal to fairly, effectively, and efficiently manage basic school operations supportive work conditions' (Bryk & Schneider, 2003, p. 42).These teachers appreciated the consistency of support over the longer term.

There was substance behind that in the actions that followed. The leaders always considered the workforce. I felt very well led.

(Neil, secondary, middle, Interview 1)

Managing workload

Support was reported as being most effective where school leaders responded to challenges of increased workloads caused by, for example, the need to develop new ways of teaching, and unpredictable absence of students and staff, by making changes which took account of teachers' circumstances and specific needs. They led in the development of policies and practices such as, flexible working arrangements; consideration of teachers' home circumstances; teachers' concerns about workload; open communication; reducing compulsory meetings. These had two positive effects: teachers felt that they benefited from practical solutions which fitted their needs, while simultaneously feeling understood, valued and trusted by leaders.

Resources were arranged to reduce workload as a result of consultation with teachers at Skyward Primary. Grace 'deliberately bought a resource', which provided ready-to use-maths videos and activities. These replaced teachers' need to create them from scratch. Her motivation for this came from genuine listening, and a concern for a teacher's wellbeing.

To begin with, she found that a bit tricky. She rang me one day from home…and she was like 'I'm working till midnight to get all these videos done'.

(Grace, primary, middle, Interview 2)

Across all schools, school leaders had taken steps to reduce compulsory meetings, particularly when teachers had tasks related to performance management.

> Having a bit of time extra after school to meet with people in your team and go through the plan of actions and has been really helpful. So, they've (SLT) stopped some staff meetings to give us a bit more time which has been helpful.
>
> *(Margaret, primary, middle, Interview 2)*

The timing of these formal commitments was also mentioned by teachers who sometimes felt leaders were 'piling it on' while workload was high.

> It doesn't take a genius to figure out 'oh hang on a minute, my teachers have got papers to mark. There's a deadline on Friday. Maybe we don't need a meeting about this right now, maybe we need to put that on the agenda for one of our inset days. Maybe this could go in an email?'
>
> *(Anna, secondary, early, Interview 2)*

Nevertheless, the same school (Greenfields Secondary) offered flexible, optional opportunities for teachers' continuing professional development.

> We've done far more optional CPD... for half an hour on Teams and I think the flexibility of that means that staff can go home quickly and then get online and do something from home. Because it's just a short bite-sized version of something it can hold their attention better. So, I think the way in which we've delivered CPD has been much better, and I can't imagine going back and not having some of that anymore and holding something altogether in the hall where everybody has to do exactly the same thing and follow it at the same pace. It seems a bit archaic now in some ways.
>
> *(Gina, secondary, middle, Interview 2)*

Cultures of trust

In a seminal research project in 400 American elementary schools in Chicago during a period of rapid reform, Bryk and Schneider identified the importance of 'relational trust' for those schools which improved (Bryk & Schneider, 2002). Relational trust relies on four conditions: 'respect, personal regard for others, integrity, and competence' (Bryk & Schneider, 2002). These echo other conceptions of trust, as having five facets: benevolence, honesty, openness, reliability and competence (Hoy & Tschannen-Moran, 1999). Relationships between colleagues and leaders characterised by high levels of trust have been identified as predictors for teacher resilience (Li et al, 2019) and retention (Torres, 2016). Leadership decisions which were based upon trust in their teachers increased teacher motivation – the energy or drive attracting someone to do something by nature (Han & Yin 2016) – and their commitment to their role and school.

Trusting relationships at work largely drowned out externally generated policy related irritations that caused many teachers to doubt their ability to live up to perceived national expectations. As Teresa stated,

102 Organisational belonging and commitment

> My concern now is children catching up and teachers being told they're not doing a good enough job ...the people that are in the government and the people that set all these standards and targets ... that's what worries me, the teachers, is that we're going to be told we're not doing this well enough. We're not doing it right.
>
> *(Teresa, primary, middle, Interview 3)*

Teresa's recovery from adversity came through the collegial nature of her relationships with colleagues at Skyward Primary.

> If any of us are struggling, we will talk to each other. And I think we're lucky because we've got that really strong team around us ... I know that we make a big difference for these children's lives.
>
> *(Teresa, primary, middle, Interview 3)*

At Sunny Hill Secondary, teachers experienced relational trust through their interactions with leaders and colleagues. Natalie's motivation to teach there emerged from her engagement with others in a continuing professional development (CPD) session.

> That CPD did what we wanted it to do – staff came out of that and said, 'I forgot why I was here. I know that's why I'm here, but it wasn't until we spoke about it, and looked at some of the research around it'...it's talking about knowledge is power and how that means we can help, with social justice, by giving children equal amounts of knowledge... and having that CPD and coming back to that just reminded and reignited in staff the reason why they do and have stayed.
>
> *(Natalie, secondary, middle, Interview 4)*

According to researchers, the first condition of relational trust, *respect*, involves recognition of the importance of the role of others, a genuine sense of listening which may involve taking the perspective of others into account in future action (Bryk & Schneider, 2002). The respect between leaders and teachers served to motivate teachers and strengthen their commitment to their school. The second condition, *personal regard*, focuses on actions which accommodate teachers' circumstances and needs.

> Expressions of regard for others in this context tap into a vital lifeline and, consequently, important psychosocial rewards are likely to result. When school community members sense being cared about they experience a social affiliation of personal meaning and value.
>
> *(Bryk & Schneider, 2002, p. 25)*

The third condition, *integrity*, was clearly evident through the perception teachers held of their leaders putting the needs of pupils first, as they were also doing. This has been found to be a driving force for teachers, motivating them to meet their pupils needs within a school which shares their priorities and passions, and some credit it for facilitating change (Anderson, 2017; Bryk & Schneider, 2002).

> Throughout the whole thing, all of the choices were made for the children, and I think that all you can ask for from school is that they put their children first.
>
> *(Lucy, primary, early, Interview 1)*

The final condition for relational trust, *competence*, involves the confidence in others' abilities to fulfil their role within interdependent roles; relational trust was conditional on everyone being able to do their job properly.

This worked both ways, and where leaders expressed trust in their teachers the value of their relationships shone through. Gina and Neil provide examples of the effect of trusting relationships at Greenfields Secondary.

> I think just trusting staff to do a job sometimes, and asking for help when you need it.
>
> *(Gina, secondary, middle, Interview 3)*

> It's central to my philosophy …trust teachers to work hard and support them as much as you can, and I think in my experience, generally they rise to the occasion.
>
> *(Neil, secondary, middle, Interview 3)*

Relational trust is not only an important resource between teachers and school leaders; it has also been found within teachers' relationships with their colleagues, pupils, and parents and carers (Bryk & Schneider, 2002). The research reported here found teachers valued their relationships with colleagues highly, and the ways in which they collaborated were an essential part of the way their school environment helped them in mediating the ongoing challenges of the pandemic.

These findings have been reinforced by many others since then (Weinstein et al, 2020, Edwards-Groves & Grootenboer, 2021; Li et al., 2019; Torres, 2016). Trust relies on a genuine commitment to demonstrate,

> moral and ethical leadership through striving to act in a manner reflective of the best interests of students. Such leadership is guided by a personal vision reflecting values such as integrity, fairness, equity, social justice, and respect for diversity.
>
> *(Davidson & Hughes, 2020, p. 1)*

Collegiality and belonging

All teachers spoke of the association between their sense of collegiality, as defined by 'the quality of the relationships among staff members in a school' (Kelchtermans, 2006, p. 221), and a sense of belonging, defined by teachers as: feeling included, respected, accepted, supported by others (Nislin & Pesonen, 2019). Organisational commitment was heavily influenced by relationships at work as they fostered a sense of belonging.

> I work with a great team of teachers and it's why I'm at the school without a doubt, because there's a lot of teaching jobs out there. The school is quite a distance from my house. It's not a particularly easy drive, but I 100% trust the colleagues that I work with. We learn from each other, and we learn through each other, and we laugh together. We cry together. We know when each other needs support.
>
> *(Michelle, primary, later, Interview 4)*

Although most teachers (31) experienced a sense of belonging within their schools, and remained committed to them, a small minority of teachers' (5) sense of belonging wavered as they became isolated from their colleagues and/or school leadership. Emma (Coalson Primary) and Mark (Greenfields Secondary) were both isolating when colleagues and pupils returned to school, due to being clinically vulnerable. Even on returning, they felt detached and separated from their school communities.

> I still feel a bit side-lined. I still don't feel as valued as I have done in the past.
>
> *(Emma, primary, middle Interview 2)*

Mark described having to adhere to safety precautions such as mask wearing while most teachers and pupils were no longer practising this.

> I felt like a bit of a lone wolf fighting against the tide.
>
> *(Mark, secondary, middle, Interview 4)*

Barbara and Theo felt distanced from their leaders at Valley View Secondary. Their sense of belonging suffered as their relationships with the head teacher and the school's senior leadership team (SLT) broke down. They both spoke of experiencing a noticeable lack of regard for their wellbeing, respect and integrity characterising these relationships.

> I don't feel there's anybody in a senior leadership position that I can talk to... they sort of nod and say 'ok'...[it is]really tough as there was no

regard for my personal well-being.... but they're not going to do anything about it. It's not that kind of school.

(Theo, secondary, middle, Interview 3)

Most teachers (31), however, drew strength from those around them within their schools, which galvanised their self-efficacy, motivation, and commitment. Belonging within the school had a profound impact for teachers, and relationships with both colleagues and leaders which were characterised by collegiality were fundamental to their sense of belonging.

I live on my own, so this has been my family. This has been my team. This has been my friendship group. This has been my social life.... They [my colleagues] have looked after me in ways that they probably won't ever realise. It's been an incredibly affirming experience to be with these people.

(Anna, secondary, early, Interview 2/3)

Interactions with leaders and colleagues boosted their investment in the joint vision and purpose of their schools.

I think I've had a really good network of teachers that I work with, and they very kindly have given me time to share their ideas of how to do things. And now school is really good because they're constantly checking, are we OK? And they're always sharing good practice from other year groups so we are able to get ideas from other places as well to see how things can be worked more efficiently.

(Samantha, primary, middle, Interview 1)

Relationships with those with whom teachers worked closely – departmental colleagues (secondary), fellow year group teachers and teaching assistants (primary) – also played a crucial role in strengthening all teachers' ability to adapt to the challenges they faced and maintain their commitment to their schools and their roles. Strong collegial ties were also associated with teachers' sense of belonging.

The support in terms of friendship, support in terms of emotional care, support in terms of checking marking, support in terms of moderating marking with me, my head of, my line manager is amazing for that.

(Anna, secondary, early, Interview 3)

Close collegial bonds aided teachers' wellbeing, as Max, at Sunny Hill Secondary explained.

106 Organisational belonging and commitment

It has been incredibly demanding. I work with someone very closely at work and we bounce a lot of ideas off each other. We try and share with each other a positive from the day and try and focus on that.

(Max, secondary, early, Interview 2)

Simultaneously, practical benefits from collegiality were important in mediating the challenges of the pandemic.

When the heads of year work so closely together, when you've got a team of staff that are singing from the same hymn sheet...that breaks problems down into smaller chunks, it makes if feel more manageable.

(Max, secondary, early, Interview 2)

Conclusion

The evidence in this chapter clearly illustrates that leadership care and support, trust, and collegiality were fundamental to teachers' sense of belonging, particularly important during those times of uncertainty which the pandemic brought.

It's like you come together, don't you? Isn't that natural when you are going through a rocky time together?

(Cate, primary, early, Interview 4)

We're always a really strong team, but now we are even stronger as a team because we've had to support people who perhaps were having a hard time.

(Dawn, primary, later, Interview 3)

If you have good relationships within the department, if you have happy staff, happy teachers, they will put in the work themselves. They will want to because they'll be enthused.

(Neil, secondary, middle, Interview 2)

Successful school leaders, particularly head teachers, are architects of relational trust (Gu, 2014) and the organisers of conditions for this to flourish (Louis et al, 2016: Gu, 2014; Tschannen-Moran, 2009; Cranston, 2011). Leaders who were prepared to make changes to accommodate teachers' needs were highly regarded and helped create an important sense of belonging for teachers. Not only did this provide practical solutions to teacher specific stressors, but it also caused teachers to feel valued and respected as an integral part of their school, serving to sustain and strengthen their organisational commitment. The strong sense of belonging to a community of colleagues expressed by almost all teachers in the research helped them to manage external threats, and to maintain their self-esteem (Collie et al., 2011; Mazereel et al., 2021), as they continued to believe that they were able to make a difference, regardless of circumstance. The psychological and practical gains from school leadership, trust and collegial relationships were important elements in enabling teachers to maintain their commitment. Ensuring teachers' individual commitment and sense of organisational belonging is an important consideration for school leaders and policy makers as they strive to resolve challenges of teacher recruitment and retention following the pandemic.

9

TEACHER PROFESSIONALISM

More than the sum of the parts

Introduction

How, then, may professionalism be defined in the context of this study? Over a period of two years these 36 teachers endured multiple challenges to their norms of practice and sense of confidence in their ability to make a difference to their pupils through who they were and what they did, as working contexts and conditions and classroom and staffroom relationships were tested as never before. In reflecting on the findings, this final chapter will show that, for the participating teachers, professionalism was more than the sum of the parts presented in each of the chapters. In doing so, it will seek to remind readers about the complexities of being a teacher in circumstances which, even at the best of times, present ongoing emotional and intellectual challenges to individual and collective educational beliefs, values, capabilities and practices, which test levels of commitment, individual and organisational identities, duty of care, wellbeing, and capacities for resilience. It will highlight how colleague relationships, school environments and organisational care for teachers' wellbeing helped to enable them to manage the turbulence and perturbations of the pandemic. It will show how, despite temporary fluctuations in their physical, psychological, and mental health, their deep sense of service survived, overlaid with an enduring sense of moral purpose and courage. The evidence shows that it was not one element that defined the competences and capabilities that defined their professionalism, but the accumulation and combinations of many: their persisting sense of moral purpose, hope, care and commitment; their abiding sense of efficacy, identity and resilience; their organisational belonging and relational trust; and, not least, their courage to teach. The chapter will conclude with a consideration of the implications of the shared experiences of the teachers for teacher educators, school and

DOI: 10.4324/9781003391661-9

schools' system leaders and policy-makers who are concerned about teacher recruitment, quality and retention.

Moral purpose: hope, care, and commitment

This research suggested that moral purposes were a defining driver of teachers' sense of self-efficacy, care, commitment and resilience. These were at the centre of teachers' understanding and application of their responsibilities to act in the broader as well as the narrower interests of the students, to continue to strive to make a difference in their personal, academic, and social development. Thus, the educational purposes of these teachers went beyond conceiving teaching only as an academic activity, instead encompassing dedication to the welfare and wellbeing of every student, regardless of personal circumstance and economic, cultural and policy contexts. The overwhelming evidence in this project was that almost all teachers pursued their work within an overall moral or ethical responsibility, striving to add value through who they were, what they were doing, and how they were doing it, especially through the support they gave to their students' welfare.

The persistence of hope

Teaching is, by definition, a journey of hope based upon a set of ideals. Almost all teachers retained their persistence to teach to their best and well, refusing to become passive 'victims' of circumstance. Instead, their work was underpinned by a strong sense of moral purpose and deep sense of hope and hopefulness. Arguably, it is hope that sustains us through difficult times and changing personal and professional environments. Having hope, it is claimed, is to possess a disposition, which results in teachers

> being positive about experience or aspects of that experience… the belief that something good, which doesn't presently apply to one's own life, or the life of others, could still materialize, and so is yearned for as a result.
> *(Halpin, 2002, p. 15)*

For Anna, a teacher in her early career phase, who 'loved' teaching, the pandemic experience was a roller coaster, consisting of 'highs' and 'lows'.

> I think most people go into education because they want a sense of purpose… And they can't see themselves in a job that isn't contributing to a wider system or to a wider sense of something…You're busy and you are stressed, but you sit back at the end of the day and you think, 'what a joy!' … If I ever get to the point when this job doesn't bring me joy, or I can't be the real me, then I need to find something else to do. And I think that the reason I am who I am is

> because of some of the harder things in my life. It doesn't get easier, but you build resilience, find resources, do your own work on yourself. And I think that has got me through this year in a way that means I can stay hopeful.
>
> *(Anna, secondary, early, Interview 1 & Interview 4)*

The evidence from this research is that teachers who sustained strong beliefs in their ability to make a positive difference to student learning, care and achievement were beacons of hope for their schools and communities.

In their writing about teacher hope, sense of calling, and commitment to teaching, Bullough and Hall-Kenyon (2011) concluded that teachers may remain hopeful even when they are not satisfied with their working conditions, but that over time such hope may be eroded, and with this erosion, they suggested, their optimism, commitment and resilience may also be diminished. Thus,

> Maintaining and deepening teachers' investment in and commitment to teaching are crucially important to improved practice and, therefore, of central importance to any successful effort at school improvement...policies which strengthen teachers' hopefulness are likely good for children.
>
> *(Bullough & Hall-Kenyon, 2011, p. 137)*

Hope 'allows blockages or problems to be perceived as challenges and learning opportunities' (Youssef & Luthans, 2007, p. 779). It is a personal disposition, but its strength also relates to teachers' workplace motivation, a determination to achieve goals, and a persistence in doing so whatever the circumstances.

Care

A concern for care was evident in teachers' statements about their working priorities during the two years of the research.

> As a whole, my motivation hasn't changed, and it won't change because I love my job. I love the children and if my motivation did change, I shouldn't probably be in the job. But it has dipped at times …There's just been really extreme highs and really extreme lows this year… If anything, I think I'm more motivated now than before Covid because I've missed out on so much time with the children and that's what we get into the job for. And I have missed a good portion of time with my whole class to watch them grow, to watch them progress or do really well. So I'm really determined to at least get to the end of this year. Having them for the whole time and really make some progress with them, not just academically but personally.
>
> *(Lucy, secondary, early, Interview 2)*

Teacher professionalism **111**

Ironically, the challenges also presented opportunities for teachers to increase the attention they were able to give to caring for the welfare and mental health of their students, as well as developing new ways of teaching and learning. *In one sense, this attention to both academic and welfare may be seen as a counter-force to the more instrumental focus that existed prior to the pandemic (though it should be noted that this has returned subsequently).*

> There is a professional obligation to negotiate the uncertainty for the children. But once the children are in, it doesn't feel any different...They need us more than ever. And there's a greater reason to be the best teacher that you can be more than ever.
>
> *(Michelle, primary, later, Interview 3)*

> Many of the children who have been in school seem to have enjoyed: the smaller class sizes, increased adult interaction, more time to talk about things that interest them, a more relaxed atmosphere, more personal space (some classrooms are very tight on space despite our school being new), an opportunity to be more creative, the chance to participate in some form of exercise every day. As a person who is wholly committed to recognising the development as a child, not just their academic performance, I feel that this has been a very precious time. However, I personally feel that the way our children are educated places too much emphasis on academic achievement and that this is detrimental to many individuals.
>
> *(Jane, primary, middle, Journal 2)*

Caring for and about their pupils and families was well-evidenced by teachers (see Chapter 7 for a detailed discussion). This ethic of service was widely evidenced in the interview and journal responses of teachers in this project. They and their schools played a hugely important ongoing, responsive role, demonstrating commitment to their pupils, their families and the wider community during the turbulence and perturbances that characterised this period of the pandemic.

Commitment

Motivating and engaging pupils are fundamental pre-requisites for teachers and their teaching, and require commitment (Schaufeli et al., 2002; Bakker et al., 2011). Research suggests that those teachers who consistently demonstrate agency, moral purpose, and resilience are more likely to feel a greater sense of sustained commitment than those who do not (Bobek, 2002; Howard & Johnson, 2004; Richards et al., 2016). However, to continue to draw on reserves of cognitive and emotional energy necessary to achieve these makes demands on teachers' personal and professional commitment, and tests their levels of individual and collective self-efficacy, commitment, identity, and capacities for resilience, as the chapters in this book demonstrate.

112 Teacher professionalism

Whilst many teachers enter the profession with a sense of vocation, committed to give their best to the learning and growth of their pupils, for some, even in normal times, their resolve may become diminished with the passage of time, changing external and internal working conditions and contexts, and unanticipated personal events. They may lose their original sense of commitment which is so intimately connected with their sense of moral purpose and professional identity, and which enables them to draw upon, deploy and manage the inherently dynamic, emotionally vulnerable, contested contexts in which they teach and in which their pupils learn. In this project, however, whilst all teachers experienced these challenges, over a period of two years, regardless of age, career phase, gender and school sector, they managed to sustain their commitment. An example of the effects that this had on the teachers was the response of two teachers, one secondary and one primary.

Theo, a secondary head of department, spoke at length during the interviews of the stresses and uncertainties brought by the pandemic – the lockdowns, the excessive in-school demands of the principal, and the inconsistency of external demands from the government. Nevertheless, although he had read of people 'abandoning the profession', even in the worst times he had never thought of doing so, despite him experiencing, 'one of the lowest times I've had working here, because SLT (Senior Leadership Team) are just piling it on' (Interview 3).

Mark, a clinically vulnerable and experienced secondary school teacher initially felt,

> just numbness in every part of my body and, I wouldn't say that the resilience had gone so far that I was to the point of giving in, but I was angry. I was angry and annoyed that I felt people weren't listening and responding to what the situation was, and what I would say is I took the extra day off, the weekend off and I had to force myself on Monday to get in front of a computer screen yet again.
>
> *(Mark, secondary, middle, Interview 2)*

However, his sense of commitment had prevailed.

> I feel a lot stronger and a bit more empowered now… I guess that backbone and the strength of having taught so many years, you just said 'enough is enough'. – I'm doing what works for me in order to have some wellbeing, but also to fulfil what the children need. I know what I need to do. I'm gonna go do it, and if anyone's not happy with this then they can speak to me when I get back into school. I'm glad that I did.
>
> *(Mark, secondary, middle, Interview 2 & Interview 3)*

Teacher qualities: efficacy, identity and resilience

Efficacy

Research has found what most teachers know from experience - that there are close associations between a sense of self-belief, a core part of healthy professional identity, and teachers' capacities for resilience.

> When faced with obstacles, setbacks, and failures, those who doubt their capabilities slacken their efforts, give up, or settle for mediocre solutions. Those who have a strong belief in their capabilities redouble their effort to master the challenges.
>
> *(Bandura, 2000, p. 120)*

Although such self-belief was severely tested during the pandemic and, as teacher reports in this book have revealed, from time to time some teachers in the project were tempted to leave their teaching careers. Yet they did not. What kept them was a combination of their belief that they could still make a difference in their pupils' learning lives. Many were supported in this by the mediating effects of school culture and their relationships with colleagues which provided a strong sense of collective efficacy, enabling them to 'mobilise their efforts and resources to cope with external obstacles' (Bandura 1982, pp. 143–144).

Identity

Sachs (2005) positioned teachers' professional identities at the core of the teaching profession. Over a career, teachers' professional role identities, their perceptions of their professional selves, may be stable or fluid, for longer or shorter periods, depending on the nature of the interactions between the social structures in which they work (Stryker et al., 2005), their perceptions of self (Burke & Stets, 2009), and how they manage the interface between these. However, for many, existing identities were temporarily and, in some cases, permanently disrupted, in the face of the onset and spread of COVID-19 which considerably increasing teachers' levels of professional unease, distress (Stets & Osborn, 2008), and confidence in their capacities and capabilities to teach to their best and well.

> It's not been easy. It was week two and I'd hit burn out point already just because when you're teaching these hybrid lessons, when you've got kids in the room and you've got kids on Teams, what does a good one look like? Where are the parameters for success? And I, perhaps problematically so, need those to feel safe and secure in my job .... the kicker has been I didn't expect it

114 Teacher professionalism

> to be assessments in the final two weeks of term. Where's the wind down? Where's the fun? Where's the joy of summer? We're dead, we're dead to the world.
>
> *(Anna, secondary, early, Interview 3)*

Nevertheless, despite her ongoing sense of frustration with the lack of recognition from the world outside school, the strong collegial relationships with colleagues in the department had reduced her sense of frustration, and after two years of struggle, Anna's sense of the importance of her work had increased.

> I think there was a sense of pulling together and rallying and knowing what needed to be done...The general frustration of feeling, in terms of morale, feeling like we have been working really, really hard for two years to make sure the schools stay open, that the kids stay safe. We've adapted in so many different ways, with technology in the classroom, with making sure we've got live lessons set up online, with making sure that kids don't miss out on work if they need to self-isolate.... Covid was perfect for that... I think for me especially, I was like 'This matters, this is vital that we keep these kids...' and it was a matter of safety. But it was also a matter of this is an important time for education. And now two years on... I don't know... It feels like... no pay rise, no thanks, no understanding that what we went through was also challenging... we forgot that there were adults that were really bending over backwards, really bending over backwards to provide an online education.
>
> *(Anna, sec. early Interview 4)*

Preserving a strong, positive and stable sense of professional identity requires ongoing emotional as well as intellectual energy, and a sense of self-efficacy and agency, allied with emotional wellbeing, are, 'factors that have a bearing on the expression of identity and the shaping of it' (Beauchamp & Thomas, 2009, p. 180). As Anna's story illustrates, professional identities are permeated, as much teaching is, by emotions. Their management is integral to sustaining a positive, stable sense of professional identity as teachers navigate the complex worlds of classroom and staffroom, learning and teaching, external expectations and the demands and uncertainties of changing contexts.

Resilience

Resilience has been defined as, 'the developed capacity to rebound or bounce back from adversity, conflict, and failure [which may overwhelm others] ... [and to] ... progress from these' (Luthans, 2002, p. 702). Over the years, interest has grown in the capacity of adults to be resilient over a career, in different contexts and in times of change. Resilience was especially important for teachers during the COVID-19 pandemic period, and in particular for those teaching in schools serving vulnerable communities, as was the case for the majority of teachers in this and other research into teachers in schools located in high need communities (Day & Hong, 2016).

Important to understanding resilience are the findings that it is a latent capacity and, 'complex, dynamic and multi-dimensional phenomenon' (Mansfield et al, 2012); and that the extent to which teachers are able to draw upon their reserves of resilience at different times and at different levels will be influenced not only by the attributes of individuals, but also by the social, cultural, policy, and school specific environments in which they work (Ungar, 2012). It may be strengthened or weakened by the quality of relationships with others, as the chapters in this book have demonstrated.

> There's a lot of uncertainty and a lot of change, and it's hard to keep up with everything that everybody wants. It feels like you're left in the dark constantly. The education sector is just left in the dark, last-minute decisions are made, U-turns.... every ridiculous decision is a blow to that, and you feel like saying 'What do you want from me?' When we were off, it was hard, because were faced with silence on live lessons, and as students weren't completing the work it was really demoralising.
>
> *(Theo, secondary, middle, Interview 1 & Interview 2)*

Being resilient means that individuals can absorb, bounce back and overcome setbacks which may threaten to overwhelm them (for example, in sustaining optimism and hope). However, to achieve this requires teachers to draw upon considerable amounts of energy that they may or may not have in reserve and in different quantities.

> It is important to note that teachers' perceived lack of emotional energy, feelings of insufficient competence or distant and acerbic attitude towards the students, parents or colleagues are constructed horizontally in schools' everyday practices. Burdening episodes are often embedded in school practices in such a way that members of the school community may not even be aware of them.
>
> *(Pyhalto et al., 2011, p. 1108)*

Writing before the pandemic, Mansfield and her colleagues (Mansfield et al., 2012) identified four inter-connected dimensions of resilience: *professional related* (e.g., commitment to students, effective teaching skills); *emotional* (e.g., bounces back, enjoys teaching, copes with job demands); *motivational* (e.g., positive and optimistic, persistent, has confidence and self-belief, maintains enthusiasm, focuses on learning and improvement); and *social* (e.g., builds and supports relationships, seeks help and take advice, have strong interpersonal and communication skills).

The quality of our relationships with other people influences how emotionally resilient you can be in the face of an emotional or physical crisis. In general, the more quality support you can draw upon from family and friends....[and colleagues]..., the more flexible and resilient you can be in stressful situations.

(https://www.mentalhelp.net/relationships/resilience)

The research reported in the chapters of this book endorses these and adds a fifth, *personal* dimension (e.g., is able to manage threats to their wellbeing from events and circumstances outside school). What was clear from the reported experiences of the teachers in this project is that the capacity to draw upon reserves of energy in order to continue to be willing and able to meet the unprecedented challenges of the pandemic was 'elastic over time' (Patterson & Kelleher, 2005, p. 6). Whilst there were fluctuations, for most teachers sustaining resilience was enabled by a combination of strong professional values, personal persistence, sustained motivation to teach to their best and well, and high levels of emotional commitment.

Wellbeing and organisational care

Health has been defined as, 'a state of complete physical, mental and social well-being and not merely the absence of disease or infirmity' (WHO, 1946).

It has been long agreed by researchers, policy makers and parents that teachers as professionals are at the heart of school performance and educational outcomes, and that their willingness, capacity and ability to teach to their best and well – to apply their values, content and pedagogical knowledge and skills – are fundamental to students' opportunities to progress and achieve. Researchers have suggested that teachers' levels of wellbeing (a combination of feeling good and functioning effectively) are closely tied to their sense of competence, autonomy, goal orientation, sense of purpose, and commitment to their schools (Brouskeli et al; 2018; Bullough & Hall-Kenyon, 2017; Kern et al., 2014; Turner & Thielking, 2019). Associations between wellbeing and higher student grade outcomes have also been claimed (e.g., Caprara et al., 2006).

European research on the impact of psychosocial hazards on teachers at their workplace found that, 'a higher job satisfaction is presumed to decrease the chances of stress' (ETUCE, 2011, p. 19) among teachers. Moreover, and perhaps not surprisingly, the same research found that the factors that had the strongest impact upon job satisfaction were 'trust and fairness' in the workplace, followed by 'sense of community', 'meaning of work', resources and 'work privacy conflict' (i.e., compatibilities or incompatibilities of working and private lives). From a socio-cultural perspective, then, school culture can play an important mediating role in building or diminishing teachers' reserves of emotional energy, as the chapters of this book have illustrated. Yet teachers cannot be expected to be impervious to changes in their own life circumstances, the demands of external policy, changing needs of school populations and school cultures, and events and experiences in their personal lives.

Being caring requires considerable emotional energy provided by teachers' resilience if their capacities and capabilities to care are to be sustained. Yet until the onset and continuation of the pandemic, teachers' wellbeing, sense of professional identity and resilience, complemented by the strength of their inner commitment to teaching was widely assumed to be the primary responsibility of the individual, rather than explicitly nurtured in any systemic or systematic way from within the school. It was evident in this research, however, that where the attitudes, dispositions and skills associated with wellbeing were being nurtured during the contexts and circumstances in which teachers had to manage themselves, their work, their pupils and often their pupils' families, these contributed significantly to their overall sense of wellbeing (see Chapter 8 for a more detailed discussion).

Teaching is essentially embedded in relationships, between teachers as colleagues, teachers and pupils, teachers and parents, and teachers and school leaders, who have a primary responsibility to establish positive teaching and learning communities in their schools and with the communities that they serve. Teachers' commitment, professional identities, resilience and wellbeing can be built and achieved through the establishment of caring and attentive educational settings in which school leaders and teachers promote positive and high expectations, positive learning environments and participate in building and sustaining collegial social communities, and supportive peer relationships.

The project provided substantial empirical evidence of the importance attached by almost all teachers to internal and external sources of support. An example of the effects that this had on the teachers in this research was the response of Samantha, a primary school teacher with nine years' experience who was deeply committed to her pupils and determined to help them to recover from lost learning opportunities, despite challenges to her own resilience.

> There are children that have come back from lockdown, that can't hold a pencil. That really motivates me to sort it out there and then.... you have to make sure you can do the best every day... I need to sometimes see my child [she had a baby at home], have a bit of a reality check, and then go back to work. ...I feel drained. I'm very tired and but I'm OK ... you just have to get through it. You just have to keep going.
>
> *(Samantha, primary, middle, Interview 3)*

What helped Samantha sustain her wellbeing were the positive relationships between colleagues.

> Everybody is really helpful...Just having lots of conversations with the team about what we need to do. I think that's really important, and I think that what we're doing is to manage our resilience... We're always

checking everyone is okay. We're always thanking our staff for working the day. We know our small circle that we work with, what their day has been like. So, we just make sure that they're OK. We just help each other.

(Samantha, primary, middle, Interview 2 & Interview 3)

Where there is a history of support in the workplace from the leadership and colleagues, it is more likely that such reserves of resilience will exist, though it should not be forgotten that extreme personal circumstances may exercise a stronger influence on some.

Conclusions: the courage of teaching

When Palmer first published his seminal book, *The Courage to Teach* in 1997, he was addressing a glaring void in the literature on teacher professionalism, by focusing on the importance of personal reflection, the role of personal lives within teacher identity, and their motivation to teach. He described courage as keeping, 'one's heart open in those very moments when the heart is asked to hold more than it is able so that teacher and students and subject can be woven into the fabric of the community that learning, and living, require' (Palmer, 2017, p. 11–12). The chapters in this book demonstrate not only the courage of individual teachers but also the powerful impact on teachers' capacities for courage of school cultures where individual and organisational trust are high, where educational values and purposes are shared, where the leadership is caring, and where relationships between teachers, teachers and pupils, teachers and parents and community are strong (Oishi, 2014).

There can be little doubt that all frontline service workers require, as a necessary part of their ability to fulfil the demands of their work and the needs of the individuals with whom they work, a considerable degree of courage. In the case of teachers, simply entering a classroom and engaging groups of pupils who may or may not wish to be there demands courage. Courage became even more important than ever, as the disruptions and perturbations of the pandemic continued, and the previous norms of teaching and learning, relationships with colleagues, and extended caring for pupils' welfare, whilst fearing for their own, became a necessity. Despite suffering the intensity of these challenges, almost all teachers in the project found the courage and capacities to stand their ground.

I think the courage for us as professionals has come when we have stood our ground on certain things that we believe must be part of our curriculum regardless of or in addition to the minimum national curriculum requirements down to things. Like planning in sessions to do with oracy and conversation. Now, if you're doing that, you can't get your spellings done, but actually I'd prefer my children to be able to communicate.

(Michelle, primary, later, Interview 4)

Five interwoven influences that singly and in combination seemed to influence these 36 teachers' courage: i) the workplace (related to their lives in school); ii) professional identity (related to their values and beliefs), iii) the personal (related to biographies and lives outside school); iv) the emotional (related to their sense of self); and v) the interaction between these and external events, circumstances and policy agendas.

> It doesn't actually matter whether I've got a tie on or a clean pair of shoes … I think it's far more about truly being pupil-focused and thinking about the long term, honest goals of education and what it means to be an educator, I guess. And it's not just about teaching to marks on a test and I've always tried to hold that philosophy myself anyway. I never wanted to be at a school where we just churn out grades like an exam factory, but I think it's really brought it to the core of what we do every day … It's far more about the pupils and their interactions and their personalities and just developing them as people. I think we've always done that and always tried to, at the very least pay lip service to that as something we talk about, but it has become quite central to what we do now, day to day, in a way that it never has before.
>
> *(Neil, secondary, middle, Interview 4)*

The optimism expressed by Neil is both an appreciation for the present but also the active seeking and actioning of new opportunities to ensure the continuing possibilities for future success. Much of the existing research in education has been carried out in contexts which were not as challenging as those experienced during the pandemic. In this new context, optimism needed to be sustained in the context of severe, ongoing threats to pupils' academic progression and welfare. Teachers in this study recognized the necessary association and interaction between the two, especially during times when contact was virtual, as challenges to maintain academic progress became far more complex, in situations that were, 'predominantly characterized by change and uncertainty' (Youssef & Luthans, 2007, p. 780).

What has been written in the pages of this book reflects much research around the world which overwhelmingly points, not only to the importance of teacher qualifications, and task and teaching knowledge, but to how their willingness, capacities and capabilities to teach well and to their best is influenced, positively and negatively by the contexts and conditions in which they teach, their sense of sustained emotional commitment, professional identity, resilience, wellbeing and the levels of support from governments, schools, parents and the media. Surveys continue to report the pressures of workloads, lack of recognition, poor leadership, student behaviour and lack of resources. In an increasing number of countries, recruitment, especially in schools serving the most disadvantaged communities, is declining, while rising mental health issues, stress and attrition levels are increasing. Yet, still, the majority of teachers continue.

120 Teacher professionalism

The evidence from this small-scale study is that the overwhelming majority of teachers continued to be optimistic, resilient and hopeful. They continued to believe in their ability to contribute positively to pupil learning, welfare and wellbeing, despite the constraints of the disruptions and perturbations imposed by the pandemic. They, and many teachers across the world, survived and thrived in challenging circumstances, with commitment and competence intact.

There may be wider implications here for university teacher educators, school leaders, and those who determine policy at local, regional (district) and national levels, and all who care about the education of children and young people in schools, which go beyond the experiences of the pandemic. If what these 36 teachers have shared is important, then pre and in-service teacher educators, supported by policy makers within and beyond schools themselves, need to take note. History tells us that issues of teacher recruitment, quality and retention are unlikely to be resolved unless school-based educators' workloads are re-imagined; that, in the knowledge that teaching is always an emotional and intellectual endeavour, their emotional wellbeing as well as physical energy, intellectual capacities and capabilities are supported; and that they need to feel confident that the provision and quality of support available in their workplace is appropriate to their individual as well as their classroom and organisational learning needs.

REFERENCES

Acker, S. (1995) Carry on caring: The work of women teachers. *British Journal of Sociology of Education*, 16 (1), 21–36.

Adler, P. S. & Kwon, S. W. (2002) Social capital: Prospects for a new concept. *The Academy of Management Review*, 27 (1), 17–40.

Anderson, M. (2017) Transformational leadership in education: A review of existing literature. *International Social Science Review*, 93 (1), 1–13.

Bailey, K. & Breslin, D. (2021) The COVID-19 Pandemic: What can we learn from past research in organizations and management? *International Journal of Management Reviews*, 23 (1), 3–6.

Bakker, A. B., Albrecht, S. L., & Leiter, M. P. (2011) Work engagement: Further reflections on the state of play. *European Journal of Work and Organizational Psychology*, 20 (1), 74–88.

Bandura, A. (1982) Self-efficacy mechanism in human agency. *American Psychologist*, 37 (2), 122.

Bandura, A. (1997) *Self-efficacy: The exercise of control.* Macmillan.

Bandura, A. (200) Self-efficacy: The foundation of agency. In W. J. Perrig & A. Grob (Eds.) *Control of human behavior, mental processes, and consciousness: Essays in honor of the 60th birthday of August Flammer* (pp. 17–33). Lawrence Erlbaum Associates Publishers.

Bandura, A. (2001) Social cognitive theory: An agentic perspective. *Annual Review of Psychology*, 52 (1), 1–26.

Barber, T. (2002) 'A special duty of care': Exploring the narration and experience of teacher caring. *British Journal of Sociology of Education*, 23 (3), 383–395.

Bauckham, I. & Cruddas, L. (2021) Knowledge-building – School improvement at scale. The Confederation of School Trusts. https://cstuk.org.uk/assets/pdfs/CST_Knowledge_Building_Whitepaper.pdf.

Beabout, B.R. (2012) Turbulence, perturbance, and educational change. *Complicity: An International Journal of Complexity and Education*, 9 (2), 15–29.

122 References

Beauchamp, C. & Thomas, L. (2009) Understanding teacher identity: an overview of issues in the literature and implications for teacher education. *Cambridge Journal of Education*, 39 (2), 175–189.

Björk, L., Stengård, J., Söderberg, M., Andersson, E. & Wastensson, G. (2019) Beginning teachers' work satisfaction, self-efficacy and willingness to stay in the profession: A question of job demands-resources balance? *Teachers and Teaching*, 25 (8), 955–971.

Blanden, J., Crawford, C., Fumagalli, L. & Rabe, B. (2021) *School closures and children's emotional and behavioural difficulties*. Institute for Social and Economic Research.

Blömeke, S., Houang, R. T., Hsieh, F. J., & Wang, T. Y. (2017) Effects of job motives, teacher knowledge, and school context on beginning teachers' commitment to stay in the profession: A longitudinal study in Germany, Taiwan, and the United States. In M. Akiba & G. K. LeTendre (Eds.) *International handbook of teacher quality and policy* (pp. 374–387). Routledge.

Bobek, B. L. (2002) Teacher resiliency: A key to career longevity. *The Clearing House*, 75 (4), 202–205.

Braun, V., & Clarke, V. (2006) Using thematic analysis in psychology. *Qualitative Research in Psychology*, 3 (2), 77–101. https://doi.org/10.1191/1478088706qp063oa.

Breslin, D. (2022) When relationships get in the way: The emergence and persistence of care routines. *Organization Studies*, 43 (12), 1869–1890.

Brouskeli, V., Kaltsi, V. & Maria, L. (2018) Resilience and occupational well-being of secondary education teachers in Greece. *Issues in Educational Research*, 28 (1), 43–60.

Bryk, A. & Schneider, B. (2002) *Trust in schools: A core resource for improvement*. Russell Sage Foundation.

Bryk, A.S. and Schneider, B. (2003) Trust in schools: A core resource for school reform. *Educational leadership*, 60 (6), 40–45.

Buchanan, R. (2015) Teacher identity and agency in an era of accountability. *Teachers and Teaching*, 21 (6), 700–719.

Buchanan, D., Hargreaves, E., & Quick, L. (2022) Schools closed during the pandemic: revelations about the well-being of 'lower-attaining' primary-school children. *Education*, 3 (13), 1–14.

Bullough, R. V. (2005) Teacher Vulnerability and Teachability: A Case Study of a Mentor and Two Interns. *Teacher Education Quarterly*, 32 (2), 23–39.

Bullough, R. V. (2019a) Empathy, teaching dispositions, social justice and teacher education. *Teachers and Teaching*, 25 (5), 507–522.

Bullough, R. V. (2019b) *Essays on teaching education and the inner drama of teaching: Where troubles meet issues*. Emerald Publishing Ltd.

Bullough, R. V. & Hall-Kenyon, K. M. (2011) The call to teach and teacher hopefulness. *Teacher Development*, 15 (2), 127–140.

Bullough, R.V. & Hall-Kenyon, K.M. (2017) *Preschool teachers' lives and work: Stories and studies from the field*. Routledge.

Burke, P. J. & Stets, J. E. (2009) *Identity theory*. Oxford University Press.

Campbell, E. (2003) *The ethical teacher*. McGraw-Hill Education.

Campbell, E. (2008a) The ethics of teaching as a moral profession. *Curriculum Inquiry*, 38 (4), 357–385.

Campbell, E. (2008b) Teaching ethically as a moral condition of professionalism. In L. Nucci & D. Narváez (Eds.) *The international handbook of moral and character education* (pp. 601–617). Routledge.

Caprara, G. V., Barbaranelli, C., Steca, P. & Malone, P. S. (2006) Teachers' self-efficacy beliefs as determinants of job satisfaction and students' academic achievement: A study at the school level. *Journal of School Psychology*, 44 (6), 473–490.

Chan, W.-Y., Lau, S., Nie, Y., Lim, S., & Hogan, D. (2008) Organizational and personal predictors of teacher commitment: The mediating role of teacher efficacy and identification with school. *American Educational Research Journal*, 45 (3), 597–630.

Collie, R. J., Shapka, J. D., & Perry, N. E. (2011) Predicting teacher commitment: The impact of school climate and social–emotional learning. *Psychology in the Schools*, 48 (10), 1034–1048.

Cooper, B. (2004) Empathy, interaction and caring: Teachers' roles in a constrained environment. *Pastoral Care in Education*, 22 (3), 12–21.

Corry, M. & Stella, J. (2018) Teacher self-efficacy in online education: a review of the literature. *Research in Learning Technology*, 26.

Cowie, H., & Myers, C-A. (2021) The impact of the Covid-19 pandemic on the mental health and well-being of children and young people. *Children & Society*, 35, 62–74.

Cranston, J. (2011) Relational trust: The glue that binds a professional learning community. *Alberta journal of educational research*, 57 (1), 59–72.

Cruddas, L. (2020) Systems of meaning: Three nested leadership narratives for School Trusts. Confederation of School Trusts. https://cstuk.org.uk/knowledge/guidance-and-policy/systems-of-meaning-three-nested-leadership-narratives-for-school-trusts/.

Davidson, F. D., & Hughes, T. R. (2020) Moral dimensions of leadership. *Oxford Research Encyclopedia of Education*. https://oxfordre-com.nottingham.idm.oclc.org/education/view/10.1093/acrefore/9780190264093.001.0001/acrefore-9780190264093-e-785.

Day, C. (2004) *A passion for teaching*. Routledge.

Day, C. (2008) Committed for life? Variations in teachers' work, lives and effectiveness. *Journal of Educational Change*, 9, 243–260.

Day, C. (2017) *Teachers' worlds and work: Understanding complexity, building quality*. Routledge.

Day, C. (2018) Professional identity matters: Agency, emotions and resilience. In P.A. Schutz, J. Hong & D. Cross Francis (Eds.), *Research on teacher identity: Mapping challenges and innovations* (pp. 61–70). Springer.

Day, C., Elliot, B. & Kington, A. (2005) Reform, standards and teacher identity: Challenges of sustaining commitment. *Teaching and Teacher Education*, 21, 563–577.

Day, C. & Gu, Q. (2010) *The new lives of teachers*. Routledge.

Day, C. & Hong, J. (2016) Influences on the capacities for emotional resilience of teachers in schools serving disadvantaged urban communities: Challenges of living on the edge. *Teaching and Teacher education*, 59, 115–125.

Day, C., Kington, A., Stobart, G. & Sammons, P. (2006) The personal and professional selves of teachers: Stable and unstable identities. *British Educational Research Journal*, 32 (4), 601–616.

Day, C., Sammons, P., Stobart, G., Kington, A. & Gu, Q. (2007) *Teachers matter: Connecting work, lives and effectiveness*. Open University Press.

Day, C. & Taneva, S. K. (2021) Policymaking in disruptive times: the development and impact of School Trust-designed policies on teacher and student outcomes. University of Nottingham. https://www.nottingham.ac.uk/research/groups/crelm/documents/policy-making.pdf.

Day, C., Taneva, S. K. & Smith, R. (2021) System leadership in disruptive times: robust policy making and enactment in School Trusts. https://cstuk.org.uk/assets/pdfs/QR_system_leadership_in_disruptive_times_report_2021.pdf.

Day, C., Simpson, A., Li, Q., Yan, B. & Ho, F. (2023) Teacher professionalism: Chinese teachers' perspectives. *Journal of Professional Capital and Community* (in press).

124 References

Denzin, N. (1984) *On understanding emotion*. Jossey Bass.

Diener, E., Oishi, S. & Tay, L. (2018). Advances in subjective well-being research. *Nature Human Behaviour*, 2 (4), 253–260.

Dray, J., Bowman, J., Campbell, E., Freund, M., Wolfenden, L., Hodder, R.K., McElwaine, K., Tremain, D., Bartlem, K., Bailey, J. & Small, T. (2017) Systematic review of universal resilience-focused interventions targeting child and adolescent mental health in the school setting. *Journal of the American Academy of Child & Adolescent Psychiatry*, 56 (10), 813–824.

Education Support (2022) Teacher wellbeing index (TWIX). educationsupport.org.uk.

Edwards, A. (2015) Recognising and realising teachers' professional agency. *Teachers and Teaching*, 21 (6), 779–784.

Edwards-Groves, C. & Grootenboer, P. (2021) Conceptualising five dimensions of relational trust: implications for middle leadership. *School Leadership & Management*, 41 (3), 260–283.

ETUCE (2011) Teachers' work-related stress: Assessing, comparing and evaluating the impact of psychosocial hazards on teachers at their workplace. https://www.csee-e tuce.org/images/attachments/WRS_Brochure_EN.pdf.

Fullard, J. (2021) The pandemic and teacher attrition: An exodus waiting to happen? Education Policy Institute. https://epi.org.uk/publications-and-research/the-pa ndemic-and-teacher-attrition-an-exodus-waiting-to-happen/.

Garbett, D. & Thomas, L. (2020) Developing inter-collegial friendships to sustain professional wellbeing in the academy. *Teachers and Teaching*, 26 (3–4), 295–306.

Gay, G. (2018) *Culturally responsive teaching: Theory, research, and practice*. Teachers College Press.

Goddard, R. D., Hoy, W. K. & Hoy, A.W. (2004) Collective efficacy beliefs: Theoretical developments, empirical evidence, and future directions. *Educational researcher*, 33 (3), 3–13.

Goleman, D. (1995) *Emotional intelligence*. Bantam.

Gov.uk (2022, 9 June) School workforce in England. https://www.gov.uk/governm ent/collections/statistics-school-workforce.

Grillo, M., & Kier, M. (2021) Why do they stay? An exploratory analysis of identities and commitment factors associated with teaching retention in high-need school contexts. *Teaching and Teacher Education*, 105, 103423.

Gu, Q. (2014) The role of relational resilience in teachers' career-long commitment and effectiveness. *Teachers and Teaching*, 20 (5), 502–529.

Gu, Q. & Day, C. (2007) Teachers' resilience. A necessary condition for effectiveness. *Teaching and Teacher Education*, 23, 1302–1316.

Gu, Q. & Day, C. (2013) Challenges to teacher resilience: conditions count. *British Educational Research Journal*, 39 (1), 22–44.

Gu, Q & Li, Q. (2013) Sustaining resilience in times of change: stories from Chinese teachers. *Asia-Pacific Journal of Teacher Education*, 41 (3), 288–303.

Halpin, D. (2002) *Hope and education: The role of the utopian imagination*. Routledge.

Han, J., & Yin, H. (2016) Teacher motivation: Definition, research development and implications for teachers. *Cogent Education*, 3 (1), 1217819.

Hargreaves, A. (2000). Mixed emotions: teachers' perceptions of their interactions with students. *Teaching and Teacher Education*, 16 (8), 811–826.

Hargreaves, A. (2001) Emotional geographies of teaching. *Teachers College Record*, 103, 1056–1090.

Hargreaves, A. (2005) Educational change takes ages: Life, career and generational factors in teachers' emotional responses to educational change. *Teaching and Teacher Education*, 21, 967–983.

Howard, S., & Johnson, B. (2004) Resilient teachers: Resisting stress and burnout. *Social Psychology of Education*, 7 (4), 399–420.

Hoy, W.K. & Tschannen-Moran, M. (1999) Five faces of trust: An empirical confirmation in urban elementary schools. *Journal of School leadership*, 9 (3), 184–208.

Hulme, M., Beauchamp, G., Clarke, L., & Hamilton, L. (2021) Collaboration in times of crisis: Leading UK schools in the early stages of a pandemic. *Leadership and Policy in Schools*, 1–20.

Kelchtermans, G. (2006) Teacher collaboration and collegiality as workplace conditions. A review. *Zeitschrift für Pädagogik*, 52 (2), 220–237.

Kelchtermans, G. (2009) Who I am in how I teach is the message: self-understanding, vulnerability and reflection. *Teachers and Teaching*, 15 (2), 257–272.

Keogh, J., Garvis, S., Pendergast, D. & Diamond, P. (2012) Self-determination: Using agency, efficacy and resilience (AER) to counter novice teachers' experiences of intensification. *Australian Journal of Teacher Education*, 37 (8), 46–65.

Kern, M. L., Waters, L., Adler, A., & White, M. (2014) Assessing employee wellbeing in schools using a multifaceted approach: Associations with physical health, life satisfaction, and professional thriving. *Psychology*, 5, 500–513.

Kim, K. R. & Seo, E. H. (2018) The relationship between teacher efficacy and students' academic achievement: A meta-analysis. *Social Behavior and Personality: an international journal*, 46 (4), 529–540.

Klassen, R. M. (2010) Teacher stress: The mediating role of collective efficacy beliefs. *The Journal of Educational Research*, 103 (5), 342–350.

Lave, J. & Wenger, E. (1991) *Situated learning: Legitimate peripheral participation.* Cambridge University Press.

Li, Q., Gu, Q. & He, W. (2019) Resilience of Chinese teachers: Why perceived work conditions and relational trust matter. *Measurement: Interdisciplinary Research and Perspectives*, 17 (3), 143–159.

Liston, D. P. & Garrison, J. W. (Eds.) (2004) *Teaching, learning, and loving: Reclaiming passion in educational practice.* Routledge.

Liu, Y., Bellibaş, M. Ş. & Gümüş, S. (2021) The effect of instructional leadership and distributed leadership on teacher self-efficacy and job satisfaction: Mediating roles of supportive school culture and teacher collaboration. *Educational Management Administration & Leadership*, 49 (3), 430–453.

Louis, K.S., Murphy, J. & Smylie, M. (2016) Caring leadership in schools: Findings from exploratory analyses. *Educational Administration Quarterly*, 52 (2), 310–348.

Luthans, F. (2002) Positive organizational behavior: Developing and managing psychological strengths. *Academy of Management Perspectives*, 16 (1), 57–72.

Lynch, K., & Walsh, J. (2009) Love, care and solidarity: What is and is not commodifiable. In K. Lynch, J. Baker & M. Lyons (Eds.) *Affective equality: Love, care and injustice* (pp. 35–53). Palgrave Macmillan.

Lyubomirsky, S., King, L. & Diener, E. (2005) The benefits of frequent positive affect: Does happiness lead to success? *Psychological Bulletin*, 131 (6), 803.

Mansfield, C. F., Beltman, S., Price, A. & McConney, A. (2012) 'Don't sweat the small stuff': Understanding teacher resilience at the chalkface. *Teaching and Teacher Education*, 28 (3), 357–367.

126 References

Mart, C. T. (2013) A passionate teacher: Teacher commitment and dedication to student learning. *International Journal of Academic Research in Progressive Education and Development*, 2 (1), 437–442.

Mazereel, V., Vansteelandt, K., Menne-Lothmann, C., Decoster, J., Derom, C., Thiery, E., & van Winkel, R. (2021) The complex and dynamic interplay between self-esteem, belongingness and physical activity in daily life: An experience sampling study in adolescence and young adulthood. *Mental Health and Physical Activity*, 21, 100413.

McCallum, F. & Price, D. (2010) Well teachers, well students. *The Journal of Student Wellbeing*, 4 (1), 19–34.

Meyers, S., Rowell, K., Wells, M & Smith, B. C. (2019) Teacher empathy: A model of empathy for teaching for student success, *College Teaching*, 67 (3), 160–168.

Moore Johnson, S. and The Project on the Next Generation of Teachers (2004). *Finders and keepers: Helping new teachers survive and thrive in our Schools*. Jossey-Bass.

Moss, G., Allen, R., Bradbury, A., Duncan, S., Harmey, S., & Levy, R. (2020) *Primary teachers' experience of the Covid-19 lockdown – Eight key messages for policymakers going forward*. UCL Institute of Education.

Mowday, R. T., Porter, L. W. & Steers, R. M. (1982) *Employee-organization linkages: The psychology of commitment, absenteeism, and turnover*. New York Academic Press.

NASUWT (2022) Teacher wellbeing survey – 2022: Your mental health matters. https:// www.nasuwt.org.uk/news/campaigns/teacher-wellbeing-survey.html.

NEU (2022) State of education: The profession (Press Release). National Education Union. https://neu.org.uk/press-releases/state-education-profession.

Nias, J. (1997) Would schools improve if teachers cared less? *Education 3–13*, 25 (3), 11–22.

Nias, J. (1989) *Primary teachers talking: A study of teaching as work*. Routledge.

Nislin, M., & Pesonen, H. (2019) Associations of self-perceived competence, well-being and sense of belonging among pre-and in-service teachers encountering children with diverse needs. *European Journal of Special Needs Education*, 34(4), 424–440.

Noddings, N. (2013) *Caring: A relational approach to ethics and moral education*. University of California Press.

O'Connor, K.E. (2008) 'You choose to care': Teachers, emotions and professional identity. *Teaching and Teacher Education*, 24 (1), 117–126.

OECD (2020) Teachers' well-being: a framework for data collection and analysis. https:// dx.doi.org/10.1787/c36fc9d3-en.

Oishi, S. (2014) Socioecological psychology. *Annual review of psychology*, 65, 581–609.

Owen, S. (2016) Professional learning communities: Building skills, reinvigorating the passion, and nurturing teacher wellbeing and "flourishing" within significantly innovative schooling contexts. *Educational Review*, 68 (4), 403–419.

Palmer, P. J. (2017) *The courage to teach: Exploring the inner landscape of a teacher's life*. John Wiley & Sons.

Paris, C. & Lung, P. (2008) Agency and child-centered practices in novice teachers: Autonomy, efficacy, intentionality, and reflectivity, *Journal of Early Childhood Teacher Education*, 29 (3), 253–268.

Parker, G. (2015) Teachers' autonomy. *Research in Education*, 93 (1), 19–33.

Patterson, J. L. & Kelleher, P. (2005) *Resilient school leaders: Strategies for turning adversity into achievement*. ASCD.

Priestley, M., Biesta, G. & Robinson, S. (2016) *Teacher agency: An ecological approach*. Bloomsbury.

Pring, R. (2021) Education as a moral practice. In W. Carr (Ed.) *The RoutledgeFalmer reader in philosophy of education* (pp. 195–205). Routledge.

References 127

Pyhältö, K., Pietarinen, J. & Salmela-Aro, K. (2011) Teacher–working-environment fit as a framework for burnout experienced by Finnish teachers. *Teaching and Teacher Education*, 27 (7), 1101–1110.

Richards, K. A. R., Levesque-Bristol, C., Templin, T. J., & Graber, K. C. (2016) The impact of resilience on role stressors and burnout in elementary and secondary teachers. *Social Psychology of Education*, 19, 511–536.

Ridley, M. (2020) *How innovation works: And why it flourishes in freedom.* Harper.

Rodgers, C., & Scott, K. (2008). The development of the personal self and professional identity in learning to teach. In M. Cochran-Smith, S. Feiman-Nemser, D.J. McIntyre & K.E. Demers (Eds.), *Handbook of research on teacher education: Enduring questions and changing contexts* (pp. 732–755). Routledge.

Ross, J. A., & Gray, P. (2006) Transformational leadership and teacher commitment to organizational values: The mediating effects of collective teacher efficacy. *School Effectiveness and School Improvement*, 17 (2), 179–199.

Sachs, J. (2005). Teacher education and the development of professional identity: Learning to be a teacher. In P. Denicolo & M. Kompf (Eds.) *Connecting policy and practice: Challenges for teaching and learning in schools and universities* (pp. 5–21). Routledge.

Schaufeli, W. B., Salanova, M., González-Romá, V. & Bakker, A. B. (2002) The measurement of engagement and burnout: A two sample confirmatory factor analytic approach. *Journal of Happiness Studies*, 3, 7192.

Seligman, M.E. (2012) *Flourish: A visionary new understanding of happiness and well-being.* Simon and Schuster.

Shaked, H., & Schechter, C. (2017) School principals as mediating agents in education reforms. *School Leadership & Management*, 37 (1–2), 19.

Skaalvik, E. M. & Skaalvik, S. (2011) Teachers' feeling of belonging, exhaustion, and job satisfaction: the role of school goal structure and value consonance. *Anxiety, Stress & Coping*, 24 (4), 369–385.

Slaten, C. D., Ferguson, J. K., Allen, K. A., Brodrick, D. V., & Waters, L. (2016) School belonging: A review of the history, current trends, and future directions. *The Educational and Developmental Psychologist*, 33 (1), 1–15.

Soini, T., Pyhältö, K. & Pietarinen, J. (2010) Pedagogical well-being: reflecting learning and well-being in teachers' work. *Teachers and Teaching*, 16 (6), 735–751.

Song, H., Gu, Q & Zhang, Z. (2020) An exploratory study of teachers' subjective wellbeing: Understanding the links between teachers' income satisfaction, altruism, self-efficacy and work satisfaction. *Teachers and Teaching*, 26 (1), 3–31.

Stets, J. E. & Osborn, S. N. (2008) Injustice and emotions using identity theory. In K. A. Hegtvedt & J. Clay-Warner (Eds.) *Justice* (Advances in group processes, Vol. 25) (pp. 151–179). Emerald Group Publishing Ltd.

Stryker, S., Serpe, R. T. & Hunt, M. O. (2005) Making good on a promise: The impact of larger social structures on commitments. In S. R. Thye & E. J. Lawler (Eds.) *Social identification in groups* (Advances in group processes, Vol. 22) (pp. 93–123). Emerald Group Publishing Ltd.

Swan, P. & Riley, P. (2015) Social connection: empathy and mentalization for teachers, *Pastoral Care in Education*, 33 (4), 220–223.

Taylor, C. (1977). What is human agency? In T. Mischel (Ed.) *The self: Psychological and philosophical issues* (pp. 103–135). Oxford University Press.

Thomas, L & Beauchamp, C. (2011) Understanding new teachers' professional identities through metaphor. *Teaching and Teacher Education*, 27 (4), 762–769.

Thomson, P, Greany, T & Martindale, N. (2021). The trust deficit in England: emerging research evidence about school leaders and the pandemic. *Journal of Educational Administration and History*, 53 (3-4), 296–300

Tirri, K. (2010) Teacher values underlying professional ethics. In T. Lovat, R. Toomey & N. Clement (Eds.) *International research handbook on values education and student wellbeing* (pp. 153–161). Springer.

Torres, A.C. (2016) The uncertainty of high expectations: How principals influence relational trust and teacher turnover in no excuses charter schools. *Journal of School Leadership*, 26 (1), 61–91.

Tschannen-Moran, M. (2009) Fostering teacher professionalism in schools: The role of leadership orientation and trust. *Educational Administration Quarterly*, 45(2), 217–247.

Tschannen-Moran, M. & Hoy, A.W. (2001) Teacher efficacy: Capturing an elusive construct. *Teaching and Teacher Education*, 17 (7), 783–805.

Turner, K. & Thielking, M. (2019) How teachers find meaning in their work and effects on their pedagogical practice. *Australian Journal of Teacher Education*, 44 (9), 70–88.

Ungar, M. (2012). Social ecologies and their contribution to resilience. In M. Ungar (Ed.) *The social ecology of resilience: A handbook of theory and practice* (pp. 13–31). Springer.

Weinstein, J., Raczynski, D. & Peña, J. (2020) Relational trust and positional power between school principals and teachers in Chile: A study of primary schools. *Educational Management Administration & Leadership*, 48 (1), 64–81.

Wenger, E. (1998) *Communities of practice: Learning, meaning, and identity*. Cambridge University Press.

Wheatley, K. F. (2002) The potential benefits of teacher efficacy doubts for educational reform. *Teaching and Teacher Education*, 18, 5–22.

Wheatley, M. J. (1999) *Leadership and the new science*. Berrett- Koehler.

WHO (1946) Constitution of the World Health Organization. Basic Documents. https://apps.who.int/gb/bd/PDF/bd47/EN/constitution-en.pdf.

Youssef, C. M. & Luthans, F. (2007) Positive organizational behavior in the workplace: The impact of hope, optimism, and resilience. *Journal of Management*, 33 (5), 774–800.

Zee, M. & Koomen, H. M. (2016) Teacher self-efficacy and its effects on classroom processes, student academic adjustment, and teacher well-being: A synthesis of 40 years of research. *Review of Educational research*, 86 (4), 981–1015.

APPENDIX 1: PUPILS ENTITLED TO FREE SCHOOL MEALS (FSM) NATIONAL AVERAGES*

average = 20–25% high = 26–45% very high = over 45%	*Primary schools (4–11 year olds)*						
	King-fisher FSM% very high	*Skyward FSM% high*	*Starling FSM% high*	*Vista FSM% high*	*Gold-finch FSM% high*	*Coalson FSM% high*	*Falcon FSM% very high*
Early Phase Gemma	–	–	Nina	Lucy	–	Cate	Isla Ava
Middle Phase	Jane	Teresa Grace	Saman-tha Mar-garet	Alan	–	Emma	Tim
Later Phase	Fern	Michelle	–	Sara	Dawn	–	–
	Secondary schools (11–18 year olds)						
	Sunny Hill FSM% – very high		*Valley View FSM% – high*		*Greenfields – FSM% - average*		
Early Phase (1–7 years' experience)	Zoe Mia Max		Patricia		Anna Kath		
Middle Phase (8–23 years' experience)	Dan Georgina Natalie		Barbara Theo Marion		Neil Mark Gina Orla		
Later Phase (23+ years' experience)	Sandra		Rose		-		

*Entitlement to free school meals (FSM) is used as a measure of economic vulnerability within the communities schools serve.

APPENDIX 2: INTERVIEW PROTOCOLS

Interview 1, Autumn, 2020, focus on biography, professional challenges and responses

1. Could you please tell me about yourself; e.g. how long you have been teaching, what is it like right now for you generally? In this school?
2. How you came to be a teacher? Are you glad you did? Are you as enthusiastic now as you were?
3. How has the last six months or so been for you?
4. What about the children/students?
5. What are the challenges Covid19 outbreak has brought in your working life?
6. What are your biggest personal challenges?
7. What are your biggest professional challenges?
8. Confidence levels in teaching and learning, regarding use of new technologies?
9. How your school responded to Covid19 outbreak?

Interview 2 Spring Term, 2021, focus on return to school following 'lockdown': pupil needs and effects on teachers

1. Please tell me about the most recent 'lockdown', and returning to school for the last few weeks of this term. How did it affect you? Was it any different from others? Was it easier to manage? If so, in what ways?
2. Now you are back in school, are you finding any differences in the motivations and engagement of the pupils you teach?
3. If so, how are these affecting you, in terms of your teaching and their learning?
4. Are you in any way concerned about being able to demonstrate the academic progress for your pupils?

5. Has there been a learning loss?
6. If so, how are you/the school mitigating/ helping them 'catch up' their 'loss of learning' over this and previous disruptions to their schooling?
7. Are there more, or roughly the same number of pupils that you teach who you would class as 'vulnerable'?
8. What are your thoughts about the ways in which the use of digital technology and 'blended learning' will be continued or incorporated into aspects of your teaching and your pupils' learning as your school returns to 'normal'? Please give examples.
9. What about having to be in school longer, and teaching keyworker pupils and others who may still be required to work at home?
10. How are you managing the demands on your resilience capacities this term? Are they the same or different from those experienced earlier?
11. What about the school support?
12. Going forward, have your motivations, aspirations as a professional, and/or classroom practices changed in any way as a consequence of the disruptions since March 2020? If so, please provide more details.

Interview 3 Summer Term, 2021, school support: 'recovery' and 'catch up pressures, work-life management and commitment

On return to face-to-face teaching and learning this term, after the Easter break

1. What did your students tell you about how they felt?
2. Have there been/do you continue to experience disruptions and continuities to your work?
3. Do you believe that recovery and catch-up are achievable for all your students?
4. Are there any groups of students where academic ('catch-up') is stronger/ weaker than others?
5. What support is the school and/or you providing for these students?
6. Are there any groups of students where wellbeing/mental health problems are being demonstrated? If so, in what ways?
7. What support is the school and/or you providing for those students?
8. What about your own wellbeing/mental health?
9. What about your work-life management?
10. How is the school supporting you?
11. Have government policies and/or the media over the last 3 months affected the way you think about yourself and what you do as a professional? Can you give any specific examples?
12. On a scale of 1-10, with 10 being the highest, do you feel as strongly committed to teaching now as you did before the pandemic? What are the positive and/or negative influences?

132 Appendix 2: Interview protocols

Interview 4, Autumn 2021, professionalism: teacher identity, resilience, wellbeing, pupil welfare and academic progress

1. How would you define the words, 'Teacher Professionalism?
2. Professionalism has also been defined as the possession of certain knowledge and skills, as autonomy, as commitment to students' learning, achievement and welfare, and as career-long learning.
    Do you agree with this?
3. Has your sense of who you are/your identity as a professional changed as a result of the experiences since March 2020?
4. Have any of (these) aspects of your professionalism been challenged over the last two years? Have some aspects been challenged more than others?
5. Please give one example of a challenge that you have managed well. Describe what happened and why.
6. Please give one example of a challenge that you have not managed well. Describe what happened and why. Describe the contexts.
7. How would you define the essential qualities of a good teacher?
8. There are several 'virtues' that research suggests good teachers possess: a Courageous Mindset, Empathy, Self-Efficacy, Moral Purpose, Sense of Equity/ Social Justice. Are these qualities which you have?
9. Please talk about how your reserves of each of these have been challenged since the beginning of the pandemic.
10. What or who has helped you sustain these in your work?
11. Which, if any of these has been diminished as a result of the disruptions of the last period?
12. What about your morale, mental health and resilience? Have these varied? How are they now?
13. What have been/is the positive/negative contributions of a) colleagues b) senior colleagues (including the principal) and c) personal friends/relations?
14. 'Catch-up', 'Learning Recovery' and 'Levelling-up' are words that policy makers often use to characterise what needs to be done by schools and teachers now. What is your view on how and to what extent your pupils are progressing since May this year?
15. What about their welfare and mental health?

Interview 5 Spring 2022, change: effects of pandemic on teacher motivation, commitment, resilience, autonomy, and school leadership

1. Has the pandemic changed the level of your commitment?
2. Has the pandemic changed the level of your motivation?
3. Has the pandemic increased your confidence in your belief that you can make a positive difference in learning and achievement of your students?
4. Has the pandemic changed the level of your capacity for resilience?

5. Has the pandemic changed how you think of yourself as a professional?
6. Has the pandemic increased your ability to be autonomous in the classroom?
7. Has the pandemic changed what it is like to work in this school?
8. What were the contributions of the school leadership to your wellbeing during the pandemic?
9. Are you a different or a better teacher than you were before?
10. Finally, can you talk a little about your educational purposes whether they have changed since the beginning of the pandemic, whether you have changed, and, if so, in what ways?

INDEX

action 73–4
activism 77
adaptation 36–7
adapting to challenge 28–40; efficacy/
  agency 35–7; fulfilling professional
  obligations 39–40; importance of
  workplace relationships 33–5; managing
  external threats 31–2; managing
  uncertainties 28–30; professional
  isolation 37–8; relationships with pupils
  32–3; student engagement 30–1
agency 34–7, 39, 70–6; and efficacy
  35–7, 70–6; importance of 69–82
aggressive behaviour 62
alienation 6
altruism 55
anxiety 34, 48, 55–6, 60, 65–6, 85, 95
applause 1
appreciation 20, 36, 51, 74, 79, 98–9, 119
aspiration 36, 80
Association of School and College Leaders 5
attrition 119
authenticity 2, 17
autonomy 2, 24–7, 116; decreased 24–6

backfilling social 'stuff' 46, 88
Barber, T. 95
behaviour management 14–15
behavioural problems 14, 21, 27
being let down by school 21–2
belonging *see* collegiality; organisational
  belonging
bereavement 11–12, 91, 95

Blanden, J. 88
bounceback 26, 114–15
British Academy 2
Bryk, A. S. 99, 101
'bubbles' 4, 6, 14, 16, 88, 90
Buchanan, R. 76, 88
building relationships 10–27; with
  colleagues/leaders 19–22; decreased
  autonomy/increased scrutiny 24–6;
  defining resilience 26–7; fluctuating
  self-efficacy 14–19; managing
  workload/wellbeing 22–3; meaning of
  teaching 11–13; support from others 10
building self-efficacy through action 73–4
Bullough, R. V. 110
burnout 17, 113

capability 35, 55
capacity for resilience 1, 38–9
care 32–3, 45–6, 97–8, 109–12; caring
  about/caring for 95–6; commitment
  to 83–96; costs of personal
  vulnerability 91–5; developing
  empathy 84–7; empathy 83–4; and
  leadership quality 97–8; moral purpose
  109–12; for pupils/families 45–6;
  putting pupils' wellbeing first 87–91
care as key purpose 11–13
caring for/caring about 11, 83–4, 95–6
catch up learning 2, 31, 45, 47, 74, 102
celebration 60
challenges 28–40; *see also* adapting to
  challenge

Index   135

changing practice 5–9
changing times 1–9; experiencing turbulence 5–9; home learning 9; lived experience 1–5
clinical vulnerability 7, 37, 72, 92–3, 95, 105, 112
cognitive energy 111
colleague support 10, 49
colleagues as family 20
collective efficacy 21, 35–7, 111, 113
collegiality 3, 20, 32–3, 104–6; *see also* organisational belonging
commitment 2, 6–8, 13, 23, 32–3, 41–3, 63–7, 83–107, 109–12; moral purpose 109–12; and organisational belonging 83–107; strengthening 63–7; to care 83–96; to core values 41–3
communities of practice 75
competence 14–15, 55, 101, 103, 108, 115–16, 120
confidence 10, 14–19, 29–32, 43–5, 51–2, 64–5, 70–73, 103, 108, 113–15; ethics of teaching service 43–5
constructive feedback 16, 90
consultation 100
context-in-action 69–70
contextual factors 75
continuing professional development 75, 101–102
coping with uncertainty 55–7
core values 41–3; commitment to 41–3
cost of personal vulnerability 23, 91–5
counter-narrative to distress 7–8
courage of teaching 91–2, 118–20
Courage to Teach, The 118
COVID-19 1–3, 7, 12–14, 17, 47, 50–1, 54–6, 58–61, 64, 70, 81, 88, 91–3
Cowie, H. 88
CPD *see* continuing professional development
creativity 32, 55
cultures of trust 97, 101–3
curiosity 17, 73

Day, C. 21
decision making 26
decreased autonomy 24–7
dedication 8, 39, 66, 109
defeat 29
defining professionalism 108–9
depression 35, 60
determination 12, 24, 32–3, 43, 52, 78, 87, 110, 120
developing empathy 84–7
developing new resources 67–8

Diener, E. 54
disadvantage 70, 79–81, 95, 119
disenchantment 5–6
disengagement 3, 98
disruption 4, 7, 14, 21, 97, 118, 120
distress 7, 70, 89, 95, 113
doubts about self-efficacy 71–3
dysfunction 35, 97

early-career teachers' perspectives 10–27
Education Policy Institute 5
Edwards, A. 70
efficacy 4, 34–7, 113; and agency 35–7; *see also* self-efficacy
effort 13, 36, 70, 97, 110, 113
embedding skills 24
embracing change 41–5
emotional challenges 26
emotional energy 111
emotional investment 79
emotional labour 10–12
emotional resilience 115–16
emotional support 46
emotional wellbeing 85, 87–91
emotional work 12, 17–18, 76–9, 96
empathy 80, 82–7; developing for pupils/families 84–7
empowerment 66, 73–4, 112
enabling opportunities for learning 81–2
enhancement of technology 3
entitlement to free school meals 5, 129
erosion of hope 110
ethics of teaching service 43–5, 111
evaluating progress 4, 11
evaluation of quality of life 54–5; *see also* wellbeing
excessive workloads 5–9
exclusion 14, 71
exhaustion 22, 27–9, 54, 57, 63–4, 98
expectations 15, 29–30, 40, 56, 59, 73, 117
experience 36, 40–41, 72–3, 117
experiencing turbulence 5–9

fairness 42, 103, 116
fatigue *see* exhaustion
fear mongering 34
feeling 'out of the loop' 37, 93
'feeling with' 84, 87
flexible working 100–1
fluctuating self-efficacy 14–19, 55–7
foodbanks 48, 80, 86–7, 95
foundation of care 83–4; *see also* empathy
free school meals 5, 129
frontline working 9, 118

136 Index

FSM *see* free school meals
fulfilment of professional obligations 39–40
furlough 80, 89
future wellbeing 11

genuine listening 99–100, 102
'good' teaching 84–6, 96
goodwill 32
Gu, Q. 21

Hall-Kenyon, K. M. 110
history of support 118
holistic learning 29–30, 80–2
home learning 9, 29, 32, 66, 88; *see also* online learning; remote learning
honesty 41–2, 60, 78, 101
hope 108–12
'how to be' 69–70
Hoy, A. W. 35
human agency 70
human interaction 8–9, 29, 33, 89, 105, 111

identity *see* professional identity
impact of pandemic 11–12, 30, 89
importance of agency 69–82
importance of trust 97–107
importance of workplace relationships 33–5
increased scrutiny 24–6
increased workload 22, 57
inner battles 60, 71
innovation 3, 74
integrity 101, 103–4
intellectual challenges 26
intention to leave 5, 7, 12, 21–3
interview protocols 130–3
investment in school 37–8, 92
isolation 5–9, 26, 28–9, 32, 36–8, 60, 95–6; professional 37–8

job loss 48, 86, 89
job satisfaction 14, 28, 55, 74, 116
journey of hope 109

kindness 42

lack of appreciation 18, 57
lack of trust 26
later-career teachers' perspectives 41–52
learning losses 43
letting parents down 17–19
letting pupils down 14–17
Leverhulme 2

limitations of going it alone 37–8
listening 86–7, 98–100; to students 86–7; to teachers 98–100
lived experience 1–5; turbulence, perturbations 2–5
lockdown 2–4, 15, 21, 24, 30–2, 38–9, 55–6, 61, 64–5, 87–90
loneliness 37, 39, 93
Long Covid 57
longevity 55
'lost' learning 24, 30–31, 38, 45, 117
loyalty 41, 49–51

making a difference 36–7, 67, 79–81
managing emotions 10–27
managing external threats 31–2
managing uncertainties 28–30
managing workload 22–3, 36–7, 57–67, 74, 100–1; strengthening commitment 63–7
Mansfield, C. F. 115
mask wearing 7, 29–31, 93, 104
meaning of teaching 11–13, 116
meanings of wellbeing 54–5
mediation 3, 39, 103, 116
meeting needs of disadvantaged pupils 15, 79–81
mental health 11, 22, 54, 77, 89
metaphor of sailing 53–4
mid-career teachers' perspectives 28–40
milestones 4
mindfulness 73–4
mistrust 31
Moore Johnson, S. 16
moral endeavour 37
moral purpose 34, 39, 41–3, 82, 98, 108–12; care 110–11; commitment 111–12; persistence of hope 109–10
morale 5–9, 20–22, 36, 59, 98, 114; threats to 5–9
motivation 2, 8–10, 12–13, 18–19, 31–2, 34–6, 65–7, 101–105
motivational resilience 115–16
mutual support 20, 27
Myers, C.-A. 88

National Association of Head Teachers 5
navigating storm 53–68; developing new resources 67–8; fluctuations 55–7; managing workload 57–67; meanings of wellbeing 54–5; metaphor of sailing 53–4
needs of disadvantaged pupils 79–81
negative effects of pandemic 5, 7, 22, 37
negative feedback 14, 17–19, 27

new ways of working 28–30
Noddings, N. 83
normality 30, 56

occupational wellbeing 53–68
Odyssey, The 53
'off timetable' 24
Ofqual 38
Ofsted 2, 57, 61
online learning 6–9, 15–16, 26–7, 29–31, 43–6, 66; *see also* home learning; remote learning
optimising communication 4
optimism 9, 19, 27, 32, 110, 115, 119–20
organisational belonging 32, 51–2, 97–108; collegiality/belonging 104–6; cultures of trust 101–3; exerting effort 97; leadership quality/care 97–8; listening to teachers 98–100; managing workload 100–1; in times of uncertainty 106–7
organisational care 116–18; and wellbeing 116–18
organisational commitment 104, 106–7
overcoming setbacks 36, 53, 113, 115

Palmer, P. J. 118
parental engagement 47
parental support 38
pastoral care 76–7
persistence of hope 109–10
personal efficacy 70
personal life circumstances 38–9
personal regard 101–2
personal resilience 115–16
personal vulnerability 91–5
perturbation 3, 5–9, 54, 67; *see also* turbulence
pinch points 30
poor pupil behaviour 10, 14, 16, 21, 27, 62, 78, 119
positive feedback 17, 19, 27, 34, 39, 90
poverty 80,, 86–8, 94
powerlessness 14–17, 19, 27, 70–71
PPA *see* preparation and assessment time
practised ethics of teaching service 43–5
preparation and assessment time 7, 63, 99
present wellbeing 11
Priestley, M. 72
professional development 16–17, 19
professional identity 28, 36–7, 69–82, 113–14, 119; emotional work 76–9; emphasis on care 69–70; enabling opportunities for learning 81–2;

importance of agency 69–82; making a difference 79–81; self-efficacy/agency 70–6; sense of 28
professional isolation 37–8
professional obligations 39–40; fulfilment of 39–40
professional resilience 115–16
professional responsibility 45, 64, 75, 90
professionalism in times of change 1–9
proxy agency 36
psychological capital 67–8
psychosocial hazards 116
psychosocial work conditions 53
putting pupils wellbeing first 87–91

quality of leadership 97–8

Rashford, Marcus 80
reassurance 17, 27, 30, 85, 100
reciprocity 12–13, 19
recklessness 5
relational trust 101–3, 108
relationships with colleagues/leaders 19–22; being let down by school leaders 21–2; supporting/supportive colleagues 19–21
relationships with pupils 32–3
remote learning 3, 74, 94; *see also* home learning; online learning
renewal of commitment 41–5; confidence 43–5; moral purpose 41–3
reserves of energy 39
resilience 2, 6, 19–20, 23, 26–7, 33, 38–9, 114–16; capacity for 38–9; teacher 26–7, 114–16
respect 41, 84, 101–4
risk assessment 9, 31
role models 13, 27, 79, 84,
'rollercoaster' effect 54, 56, 109–10
rudeness 15, 78

Sachs, J. 113
safeguarding 77
safety restrictions 29, 39, 70–1, 81, 104
Schneider, B. 99, 101
school culture 116–17
scrutiny 24–6; increased 24–6
self-belief 113, 115
self-doubt 14–17, 27, 70, 81
self-efficacy 10, 14–19, 23, 35–7, 39, 67, 70–6, 105, 108; and agency 70–6; building through action 73–4; doubts 71–3; fluctuating 14–19; letting parents down 17–19; self-doubt 14–17; working with colleagues 74–6

138 Index

self-esteem 55, 78–9, 99, 107
self-reflection 17, 73–4
self-regulation 74
self-renewal 36
Seligman, M. E. 55
SEND *see* special educational needs and disabilities
senior leadership team 22, 31, 51, 60, 92, 99–101, 104, 112
sense of calling 110; *see also* vocation
sense of community 27, 49, 116
sense of professional identity 28
sense of purpose 63, 66, 87, 98, 108, 112, 116
shielding 2, 37, 60, 92–3, 104
sleep deprivation 23, 39
SLT *see* senior leadership team
social capital 32, 67–8
social distancing 29–30
social isolation 28–9, 32
social resilience 115–16
social wellbeing 87–91
Soini, T. 55
solidarity 45
Song, H. 55
special educational needs and disabilities 89
strengthening commitment 63–7
'Strengths and Difficulties Questionnaire' 88
stress 5–7, 18, 22–3, 27–8, 50–5, 60–63, 116–19
struggle 1, 5, 8, 11–12, 27–8, 63, 72–3, 88–91
student engagement 4, 28, 30–1
subjective wellbeing 14, 32, 53–68
support 10, 19–21, 47–8; for more vulnerable 47–8; supporting/supportive colleagues 19–21
sustaining resilience 33

Taylor, C. 70
teacher agency 72
teacher persistence 35–6
teacher professionalism 25, 108–20; courage of teaching 118–20; defining professionalism 108–9; moral purpose 109–16; wellbeing/organisational care 116–18
teacher qualities 113–16; efficacy 113; identity 113–14; resilience 114–16
teachers' resilience 26–7

teaching as service 41–52; care for pupils/families 45–6; loyalty to school 49–51; renewal of commitment 41–5; sense of belonging 51–2; support for more vulnerable 47–8
Teams software 2
thirst for knowledge 30
threats 5–9, 31–2; managing external 31–2
traits of successful teaching 35–6
trauma 11, 26–7, 77, 90–91
trust 26–7, 37–8, 87, 97–108; cultures of 101–3; lack of 26
Tschannen-Moran, M. 35
turbulence 2–9, 67; experiencing 5–9; and perturbations 2–5

uncertainties 28–30, 35, 55–7, 106–7; coping with 55–7; managing 28–30; trust in times of 106–7
understanding 'how to be' 69–70
unprecedented challenge 97
unpredictability of government decisions 29, 38, 61

value of intentions 70
victims of circumstance 6, 8, 109
virtual meetings 17
vocation 55, 67, 110
vulnerability 3–4, 7, 15, 29, 47–8, 77, 81, 85–8, 91–5; costs of 91–5

wellbeing 11, 22–3, 53–68, 87–91, 116–18; meanings of 54–5; occupational/subjective 53–68; and organisational care 116–18; putting pupils first 87–91
wellbeing committee 50–1
Wellbeing Wednesdays 60
work performance 55
work-related stress 5
working with colleagues 74–6
working from home 29, 58–9, 93–4
workloads 5–9, 22–3, 57–67, 100–1; excessive 5–9; managing 22–3, 100–1; strengthening commitment 63–7
workplace relationships 33–5; importance of 33–5
work–life management 49, 99
work–privacy conflict 116

zombies 31

Printed in the United States
by Baker & Taylor Publisher Services